THE GLASGOW
HERALD
BOOK OF
SCOTLAND

THE GLASGOW
Herald

BOOK OF
SCOTLAND

Edited by

ARNOLD KEMP

and

HARRY REID

MAINSTREAM
PUBLISHING

First published in Great Britain 1990 by
MAINSTREAM PUBLISHING COMPANY
(EDINBURGH) LTD
7 Albany Street
Edinburgh EH1 3UG

British Library Cataloguing in Publication Data
The Glasgow Herald Book of Scotland. – (Glasgow
    Herald series).
  1. Scotland
  I. Kemp, Arnold   II. Reid, Harry   III. Series
  941.10858

ISBN 1 85158 352 1

Design and finished artwork by
James Hutcheson and Paul Keir

Typeset in 10/11 Garamond by Bookworm Typesetting
  Ltd, Edinburgh
Printed in Great Britain by Butler and Tanner Ltd,
  Frome

Contents

This book is dedicated to all Glasgow Herald *photographers, past and present. We wish to thank the* Glasgow Herald *Picture Desk and Outram Photo Librarians for their marvellous co-operation in the production of the* **Glasgow Herald** *Book of* **Scotland.**

Introduction

SAATCHI AND SAATCHI COULD NOT HAVE DONE BETTER. THE KILTED KIN wore flesh-coloured tights and short tartan stockings. Hanover embraced the Highlands in the shadow of Holyrood.

The occasion – George IV's visit to Edinburgh in 1822, so skilfully and ludicrously stage-managed by our very own Sir Walter Scott – must have been a traumatic experience for the lowland citizens of the nation's capital. Suddenly tartan was in and *all* historical logic was out. Jacobitism was embraced by the Crown! To a people already predisposed to a Calvinist-induced dichotomy (in the blue corner, weighing in at several stones of hypocrisy, the Elect; in the red corner, carrying the burden of a nation's history, the Damned) this Royal visit simply served to confuse further. Scottish or British? Romance or History? The duality has been passed down through generations.

I can't remember when I first realised I was a Scot. I do remember a stirring of resentment at another Royal visit – to Kilmarnock in the 1950s – when we primary school kids were handed miniature Union Jacks to wave as Her Majesty passed the school gates. As we lined the pavements we were informed that the Queen's automobilised cavalcade was on its way up Dundonald Road and would pass us in just a few seconds. A teacher inspired hurrahing and clapping began. Looking down the street I was suddenly transfixed by the grandest vehicle I had ever seen, gleaming blue and gold on a dull Ayrshire day. I cheered and cheered as Murdoch's potato lorry passed and gave no notice whatsoever to the line of black limousines which had accidently preceded. I hasten to add that I put my seemingly insouciant actions of that day more down to youthful naïvety than to any smouldering republican nationalism but like the good burghers of Edinburgh in 1822 I was confused.

This national identity crisis, which in some individuals can be telescoped into a kind of tartan angst, an anarchic duality which veers wildly from assertion to negation, affects all aspects of Scottish culture. Fortunately it also does much to dictate our sense of humour and irony. In a recent Edinburgh Festival radio programme I heard the members of the *Scotland the What?* comedy trio asserting that the name of their act was inspired by their collective incredulity of the sentiments expressed in a song which was at that time sweeping the nation – 'Scotland the Brave'. Scotland the what . . .? I don't believe any of us could actually ever have considered membership of the White Heather Club and I refuse to believe that the performers who make a living by swinging their kilts at those desperate, ersatz city hotel 'ceilidhs' really take it seriously.

Then again, maybe I'm wrong. From where I sit it sometimes appears that the only growth industry in Scotland is to be found on the heritage trail. The question is: whose heritage? We build pit museums and close pits; our industrial inheritance is unemployment. While Glasgow trumpets its year as European City of Culture and a new renaissance of belief in the Dear Green Place, down the road in Greenock they're raising the begging bowls to toast their bottom placing in a recent UK-wide survey of economic deprivation. While Aberdeen and the North-East can look forward to another decade of oil-fired affluence, the Highlands – those wee bit hills and glens we can become so sentimental and maudlin over with the aid of our usquebae – are being transformed into some junked-up tartan theme park; and meanwhile the hills are alive with the sound of Dutch, Arab and English owners warning Highlanders to keep off the grass. Edinburgh continues to debate its phantom of an opera house without reference to the guid people in the housing estates where the tourist buses never go.

The contrasts are an inherent part of Scotland today. We can scale the emotional Nevises through a truly awesome rendition of 'Flower of Scotland' from the Murrayfield stands; we can be moved by the thought of MacDiarmid's little white rose of Scotland 'that smells sharp and sweet – and breaks the heart'; we can dance furious Highland flings of national conceit from Hong Kong to Govan ('Wha's like us?'); but we can also plumb depths of North Sea dimensions with our communal insecurity and our brooding sullen resentment of our own powerlessness.

This book, itself a product of a continuing fruitful relationship between the *Glasgow Herald* and Mainstream Publishing and lavishly illustrated with old and new photographs from the famous Outram Picture Library, is about being Scottish, about living in Scotland in all its myriad identities and manifestations. It is both a celebration and a challenge and it is written by some of the best minds in Scotland today. Hopefully it will serve to lessen the confusion.

Bill Campbell
Mainstream Publishing
Edinburgh
September 1990

ARNOLD KEMP

Big City Rivalry

Glasgow and Edinburgh

THE GREAT RIVALRY BETWEEN EDINBURGH AND GLASGOW, ONE OF THE
fixed points of Scottish life, has survived an intensified proximity. Roads now
link the cities in less than an hour by car and the rail service, on its better days,
cuts the journey between them to a time that in London would be regarded
as a mere instant in a commuter's day. Many people do live in one city and
work in the other, a fact that makes the rail route a curiosity of European
railways – a busy line on which people simultaneously travel to work in both
directions. Yet the acid of jealousy still drips. Edinburgh may acknowledge
Glasgow's enterprise and ambition, drawing unfavourable comparison with
its own erratic history of civic leadership, but Glasgow's cultural pretensions
are quietly derided as cosmetic or faintly ludicrous. Glasgow acknowledges
and admires Edinburgh's spectacular beauty but finds the capital's stolid air
of superiority irritating and complacent. Both cities are reluctant to give up
cherished myths about each other.

There is a school of argument which deplores the rivalry and believes that
the two cities should work together, for example in the promotion of tourism
and the arts. Like many other admirable sentiments it has little popular
currency. But the rivalry, if sometimes petty and based on groundless
assumptions, is also dynamic. All the great cities of the world owe much
to ambition: in the inherited architecture of Edinburgh and Glasgow there
is ample evidence of that. Edinburgh may be reluctant to acknowledge any
debt to Glasgow, but without Glasgow's revival in the 1980s it is certain that
Edinburgh would have been slumbering still. Edinburgh has been *provoked*
by Glasgow into a more aggressive frame of mind.

After a career mostly spent on Scotland's two serious morning newspapers
– first in Edinburgh and, for almost the last decade, in Glasgow as editor of
the *Herald* – the nuances in the relationship between the two cities continue
to fascinate me. Edinburgh people still ask: *And do you live in Glasgow?*
Behind the question lies the implicit comment that moving to live (rather
than work) in Glasgow is strange and eccentric. It is true, of course, that
Edinburgh has been more successful than Glasgow in preserving its centre
as a place in which to live as well as to work. The post-war bout of
slum-clearance and demolition had different consequences in each city. In
both, the poor and the deprived were banished to the new peripheral housing
schemes that are now recognised as one of the major blunders of the period.
But whereas Glasgow embraced the urban motorway, Edinburgh rejected
it after one of the early environmental battles. The Edinburgh bourgeois
property-owner remained in control of the central areas. Commerce captured
only the heights of the New Town, leaving the lower slopes to domesticity,
and, viewed from Blackford Hill on a sunny day, the south-side mansions,
in their orderly avenues, remain the essence of harmonious prosperity ten
minutes from Princes Street. The centre of Glasgow was abandoned by its
middle class, who decamped to spacious suburbs mostly outside the city's
administrative boundary. The grandiose Victorian domestic architecture at
the western end of Sauchiehall Street or up on the hill around Park Circus

Park Circus,
Glasgow, 1989.

was given over almost completely to business. Large parts of the West End, with their enormous Victorian and Edwardian terrace houses, were left to be divided into flats by developers. Glasgow is just getting over the furious bout of demolition that persisted into the 1960s. Only in the last decade or so has restoration begun to reclaim the fine old tenements and private building to fill the gap sites with *bijou* apartments. Animation has returned but when I tell my Edinburgh friends that I *enjoy* living in Glasgow their surprise, though polite, remains unmistakable.

It is simplistic to say that Glasgow is a working-class, proletarian city, whereas Edinburgh is bourgeois. Yet, like all generalisations, it has an essence of truth. Glasgow's industrial past has left its stamp everywhere, whether physically in the commercial architecture and the monumental cranes on the river, or intangibly in the hearts and minds of the immediate post-industrial generation. A curious theme has emerged in the new Glasgow literature and among artists and intellectuals, of regret and anger at the loss of a tradition that had dignity and toughness. Writers like William McIlvanney and Peter McDougall still mine that seam in novels and plays, of course, but others deplore its transformation into an economic culture that they find demeaning and exploitative and even wimpish, a Glasgow not of dungarees and cloth caps but of designer clothes and expensive hairstyles. In my view Glasgow had very little choice but to seek substantial public funding to restore its fabric and turn itself from a self-contained industrial city into a service and tourist centre dependent on external investment, retail commerce, tourism, the arts and leisure. As an incomer, perhaps I find this easier to accept because I am not so keenly aware of what went before. For people born and brought up in Glasgow, especially among its sometimes sullen intellectual class, there is often a sense that the city has been stolen from them. The new service sector, they point out, pays slave wages. The work in it has no future. The culture celebrated during 1990, when Glasgow somewhat to the annoyance of Edinburgh won the title of European City of Culture, was imported and alien. The opera company, the theatres, the museums and art galleries were in the hands of outsiders and carpetbaggers. Nowhere have these feelings been more strongly evident than in the controversies over the future of Glasgow Green and the People's Palace. The city's proposal to turn part of the Green into a leisure park has enraged those for whom it is more than the very heart of the Dear Green Place. For them it is scene and symbol of a popular political tradition and radical protest going back to the earliest industrial times. Official neglect of the People's Palace, and the shabby treatment of its curator Elspeth King, who over a period of 16 years has developed what is regarded as an outstanding museum of social history, have fed the anger of this dissident group, allying it somewhat uneasily to Ms King's army of less politically motivated supporters who greatly admire her work and achievement. It has also brought it into sharp conflict with the machine Labour politicians who run Glasgow from the ornate magnificence of the City Chambers created by the merchant class at the height of Glasgow's mercantile self-confidence.

Opposition to the development of the Green – which would, in the scornful phrase of the protesters turn part of it into a 'Disneyland' – arouses intense impatience in the ruling Labour group, where pragmatism is the order of the day. 'All they want to do is to keep Glasgow Green free for a riot every 20 years,' an official told me contemptuously. It is true there is an emptiness in some of the protests for they do not offer any positive alternatives to Glasgow's chosen course. The old industries will never return and you might ask if we should lament their passing quite as much as we

BIG
CITY
RIVALRY

12

Charlotte Square,
Edinburgh, 1989.

*Cricket on Glasgow
Green, 1989.*

do. Their wage-slavery was as real as anything in the bars and bistros of the Merchant City. The trade unions born to prevent exploitation themselves became corrupt, masonic and a source of sustained religious, ethnic and sexual discrimination. The industrial legacy includes a pernicious impact on public health that still leaves Glasgow with an appalling record in the league tables of cancer and heart disease, probably closely derived from diet and life-style. Given Glasgow's emotional and political baggage, the most remarkable aspect of its revival has been the political alliances that have been formed in a city which was divided not only by class but by religious and ethnic origin. The Highland and Irish strains in Glasgow have given it much of its dash, colour and love of live music, and have led to a Labour-Catholic dominance of the district council. Their electoral pre-eminence reflects not only Conservative unpopularity in Scotland but also the retreat of the Protestant middle-class to the suburbs. The prudent district councils round the periphery show little flair and work hard to keep the poll tax down through careful management. But the civic leadership in George Square has forged a strong partnership with the largely Protestant business groupings in Glasgow, who come down from a long line of Hanoverians. This new friendship has been lubricated by substantial public funding, mostly channelled through the Scottish Development Agency, and if its first motives were those of self-interest, it seems to me to have grown during the 1980s into something more – a genuine pride in the city's recovery, a mutual respect, and a desire to work together. It is not surprising that this pragmatic Labour leadership should have stirred up hostility among its political purists.

Similar tensions have been evident in Edinburgh, of course. The festival was started after the war in a notable act of civic ambition but thereafter it began to wither on the vine. Conservative (or Progressive) administrations could find little enthusiasm for the expenditure required to sustain the festival and it was reviled by many Labour politicians as elitist. When Labour came to power in Edinburgh the festival went through an unhappy and insecure period. The solid Edinburgh bourgeoisie have year in and year out been faithful supporters of festival and fringe, contrary to some of the sneers from London newspapers, but their support has not been unanimous. Some have made a point of leaving the city to avoid the festival. Others curse its tourist influx, blaming it for promiscuous influences which led Edinburgh to become a centre of drug-addiction and the Aids capital of Europe. However, the Labour administration has now become reconciled to the festival. Like its counterpart in Glasgow, it recognises the importance of the arts as a means of sustaining employment in the service industries, and the hard fact is, as Glasgow's Labour leader Pat Lally has pointed out, that funding for more obviously social programmes, like housing, would simply not have been available. His message, that the available funds should be exploited as much as possible, has now been accepted in Labour local government circles in Edinburgh and elsewhere.

Glasgow is hydra-headed, like a cauliflower. In its power system the most important elements are the City Chambers and the Merchants House, whose partnership we have noted. Edinburgh is like an onion, composed of concentric layers. At its heart is the law. The outer rings begin with the senior civil service, the universities and the financial community. The Treaty of Union preserved the law and the church among Scottish institutions. The church has languished in a secular age but the law has preserved its power and its privilege. The supreme courts usurped the seat of the old Scottish Parliament and the gowned advocates saunter in the old Hall with a complacency that some find arrogant. These men, these judges, these silks,

*'Smart boy . . .
That's me, Missus.'
An old newsagent's
shop at the People's
Palace, Glasgow,
1983.*

*Damien Faulds
rehearses for the
Feea festival, at the
Nelson Monument,
Glasgow Green,
1989.*

these advocates, these juniors, these clerks and custodians, are drawn from a small circle. Sometimes I think the judges and advocates all went to my old school, the Edinburgh Academy. The classic route is Oxbridge and then Edinburgh University. Many lawyers outside Edinburgh think these men are grievously out of touch with the world. Certainly, when Lord Hope, the new Lord President, in 1990 gave an extraordinary briefing to the press in the hope of ending rumours of a homosexual ring on the bench, he behaved with a simplicity, one might say a naïvety, that was staggering. He called editors or their deputies to his New Town house. There was no security and only the most cursory request for identification. There were no information officers, no experts in the modern art of public relations. Lord Hope sat at the head of his study table with his clerk behind him in the window. So convinced was I that we were to be given the off-the-record intimidatory warnings the Scottish press has come to expect in its dealings with the judiciary that I had not even brought a notebook, and had to improvise with a chequebook and borrowed implements. We were asked to swear that we would treat what Lord Hope said as non-attributable. We all raised our hands and so swore. He then attempted to dispose of allegations of homosexual misconduct involving five judges, of whom one had resigned. He named none of the others but assigned them all letters of the alphabet – Judge A, Judge B, and so on. No sooner had I been released and returned to Glasgow, than my phone rang. It was a London newspaper, asking for an account of the meeting. So much for the oath to which we had all sworn; the meeting was by now an open secret at Westminster and on the news desks of Fleet Street. I stuck to my undertaking but others did not and a pretty complete account of the meeting eventually surfaced in the press. After an enormous splurge of publicity, the matter died, and so Lord Hope, through naïvety or perhaps a devious skill with which he is not credited, achieved his purpose. But in so doing he enraged his fellow judges and left the Scottish bar in a profoundly demoralised state.

Scots law can always be sure of a thriving criminal practice. After all, we put more people into jail per head of population than any other civilised country in Europe. In that respect our productivity is *excellent*. But Scots mercantile law is in decline. On actions for damages the Scots courts are being bypassed wherever possible because of their niggardly awards. And access to European litigation is largely organised through London. In one of the most curious parliamentary episodes in recent times, Scotland's otherwise comatose Tory MPs organised a rebellion which stifled the reforms designed to introduce in Scotland free-market principles that had already been agreed for England. Ravenscraig may close; Scottish emigration may accelerate; but the Scots lawyers are saved again, even if saved only to disport themselves in a protected backwater.

If you are looking for the quintessential difference between Edinburgh and Glasgow you need look no further than the law. The Edinburgh judge or advocate is securely ensconced. He is a member of our most privileged elite. Anyone pursuing an action at the Edinburgh courts must brief an Edinburgh solicitor. What with conveyancing, a certain amount of criminal work and the dripping roasts of trusts, your average Edinburgh solicitor has acquired a genteel and comfortable manner. He does not have the sharpness of your Glasgow solicitor, who has to live on his wits. Indeed he cultivates a more gentlemanly air. Edinburgh lawyers look down on their Glasgow counterparts who, they think, dress loudly and may have unsuitable accents. They did not always go to the right school. And it has to be admitted that whereas Edinburgh legal dinners, as far as I know, have always been the

Demonstrators after the opening of the West Flank Ring Road, Glasgow, 1972.

Festival time,
Edinburgh, 1989.

models of decorum, the annual dinner of the Glasgow Bar Association has always been notorious for its uninhibited character. To say that bread rolls are thrown, as at the Drones Club, is an understatement, and there is nowhere in Glasgow more convivial than Babbity Bowsters when the lawyers meet to trade the latest gossip from the courts.

Glasgow is indeed a more raffish and flashy city. To that extent the myths are true. It is indeed a more working-class city, in that its middle class is relatively smaller than in Edinburgh. Yet Glasgow's middle class is no less intensely respectable. In some parts of the south side respectability could hardly be given a higher value. Glasgow, with its Italians, its Asians, its Jewish population and its remarkable concentration of professional musicians, is also, without doubt, more cosmopolitan. If you go to a party in Glasgow you are likely to find at least someone who can sing or play well, or both, and a song needs little provocation. Glasgow is not an ugly city. Indeed, those who know it come to find it beautiful, full of unexpected townscapes. But it is not continuous or harmonious. Edinburgh is one of the best-preserved urban environments in Europe. Its beauty is often of extraordinary power but its schizophrenic nature, so much a part of its mythology since Deacon Brodie inspired Jekyll and Hyde, is unabated. In the old days, of course, its architecture formalised that schizophrenia, for in the interstices of the New Town, between the elegant broad terraces, there were noisome lanes of tenements for the poor. Now they too have been gentrified where they have not been swept away. There is a new dimension to the schizophrenia: not only do we have the contrast between the genteel and the vulgar, between Morningside and Pilton, but now we have the contrast between the Scots and the English. Edinburgh is a more highly anglicised city than it was and than Glasgow is now. Glasgow, of course, has thought of itself not as Scottish but as *Glasgow sui generis*. In Edinburgh, with its memorials of vanished political power, it is impossible to avoid a pervading sense of Scottishness under challenge. It was in response to that that the *Scotsman* newspaper in the 1970s became so stridently devolutionary and now that this movement has for the moment failed, the paper must steer a new course somewhere between the Olympian generalities of the London journals (under which English nationalism lurks) and a Scottishness that does not grate in a city that regards the term *parochial* as a dirty word, a curious way of looking at your own life.

The street in which I grew up so happily, on the northern fringe of the New Town, did have its English residents in my young day. They fitted easily into this bourgeois milieu. Now that graceful street beside the Water of Leith is, as far as I can make out, mostly occupied by people from the South. The reasons for this are not hard to understand. Most of the professions, with the exception of the law, are organised on a UK basis. The universities, the arts and the financial community are obvious examples. Scots students may still lodge in Marchmont but some of their richer English colleagues can afford New Town flats. Even the law, Edinburgh-style, has had something of a tendency to ape English manners. This process of change cannot be resisted. We cannot be surprised that Edinburgh's beauty and its outstanding quality as a liveable city attract people to it. The process has welcome elements. It has expanded our horizons, it has brought new perceptions, tastes and attitudes. Underlying it are more disturbing social changes which are not confined to Edinburgh, or Scotland. They are to be found throughout Europe where indigenous populations, living in relative poverty, emigrate and are replaced by a secondary population who have accumulated superior wealth in metropolitan centres where they find life increasingly unpleasant.

Festival time, Edinburgh, 1989.

Law Glasgow-style –
Joe Beltrami, 1988.

Law Edinburgh-style
– the annual
'Kirking' of the
Court, St Giles,
Edinburgh.

It would be surprising if social tensions did not result, not just because of the impact on property prices.

Yet the old demotic spirit of Edinburgh is still there. The people perhaps have not changed as much as one sometimes imagines. When Mr Wallace Mercer, the chairman of Hearts, produced his plan to merge his club with the Hibs by dint of taking them over, he was shocked by the popular outrage that resulted. I am glad that Hibs have survived not just because I grew up as a Hibs supporter and have affectionate memories of Easter Road but because local rivalries, like the rivalry between Edinburgh and Glasgow, have positive as well as negative qualities. They produce loyalty and energy and the spirit of emulation. Out of these qualities excellence can grow. And as long as the ordinary people of Edinburgh survive they will go on confounding another myth sometimes nurtured by Glasgow – that of their *east-windiness, fur coats and no drawers, ye'll have had yer tea*. In all my many years in Edinburgh I encountered nothing but kindness and good humour from my neighbours and help in times of need. There is nothing wrong with the folk of Edinburgh. They are more reserved, perhaps, than Glaswegians, not so instantly voluble. Perhaps they are a little cannier, less easily enthused and less prone to despair. They may prefer the crumpled tweed to the designer jacket. Perhaps Edinburgh is prone to contemplate itself in the glass and pronounce itself excessively pleased. Perhaps Glasgow, with the cheek of the butcher's dog, shouts too much about its own merits. But long live Edinburgh and Glasgow, and long live their rivalry.

The Auld Enemy

Scotland and England

IN JOHN BUCHAN'S SUPERB STORY *THE THIRTY-NINE STEPS*, RICHARD
Hannay, after his adventures in the hills of Southern Scotland, escapes
from the Black Stone – the baddies – and arrives in Berkshire where he
is to make contact with Sir Walter Bullivant, the mandarin who represents
order, security and the forces of good.

After his desperate escapades on the exposed uplands of Scotland, Hannay
makes contact with Bullivant by the douce banks of the River Kennet.
Buchan goes out of his way to emphasise the contrast:

> After Scotland, the air smelt heavy and flat, but infinitely sweet, for the
> chestnuts and lilac bushes were domes of blossom. Presently I came to a
> bridge, below which a clear slow stream flowed between snowy beds of
> water-buttercups. A little above it was a mill; and the lasher made a pleasant
> cool sound in the scented dusk. Somehow the place soothed me and put me at
> my ease.

*Lord Tweedsmuir
(John Buchan),
Governor-General
of Canada, wearing
Indian head-dress,
Calgary, 1936.*

I first read this as a young boy, well before I ever went near England.
All I was aware of then was the very strong physical contrast between the
Kennet and the upper Tweed, where Hannay had concluded his adventures
in Scotland. Now, in cynical middle age, I read more into the passage; here
is the subconscious of Buchan, the Scottish anglophile *par excellence*, linking
England with sweetness and indeed salvation.

Buchan spent his adult life away from Scotland. He was a classic exemplar
of the Scotsman on the make, working his way up through the institutions
of the Empire and the English establishment. He is typical of a certain Scot
who sees his career, even his destiny, lying furth of his native land. Such is
the pull of our more powerful neighbour.

Our problem has been, for many, many centuries, that the English *are*
more powerful, in almost every way that counts – financially, politically,
culturally, internationally. Only in terms of individual achievement – the
Scots are far more ingenious, more inventive, and more imaginative than
the English – have we more than held our own. The Act of Union in 1707
was allegedly about a union of equals, but the reality was the English could
smash it with impunity. They did so just five years after it was signed, on the
vexed issue of lay patronage in the Kirk.

The great tragedy of Scottish history is that it need not have been thus. The
English have treated us badly over the centuries, but they could have been
much worse. And we have had our chances to come to a pragmatic and even
advantageous accommodation with them. We threw them all away.

One classic example came in 1503. Henry VII of England wanted to have
good – permanently good, he was no short-term opportunist – relations with
Scotland. He didn't like Scotland's Auld Alliance with France. (The Scots
should not have liked it either; as Allan Massie has correctly pointed out,
we never gained any political or economic advantage from it.)

Anyway, Henry wanted to marry his daughter Margaret to James IV
of Scotland. This was a far-sighted and potentially momentous initiative.

James dithered; he was, erroneously, less convinced of the benefits of stable relations with the English. But eventually he concurred. The marriage arrangements were dealt with by the great Scottish poet William Dunbar, and the 14-year-old Margaret was welcomed over the Border by the Archbishop of Glasgow and a throng of cheering Scots. She moved on to meet James at Dalkeith. This should have been one of the most joyous and significant episodes in our history.

Yet James boorishly snubbed her at the wedding; she was not allowed to eat until the second sitting, by which time James had already dined with the archbishops of Glasgow and York. Later he lavished attention on his male cronies, and he would parade his mistresses before his young queen. Nevertheless the marriage was, at the personal level, a success, and Margaret bore James six children.

But it was not a success in the way Henry had wished. James may have been Scotland's greatest-ever monarch, but he lacked the vision and pragmatic adaptability of Henry. (Even allowing for their advantages in terms of wealth and population, the English have always been better at politics than the Scots. They are better at compromise, they are good committee men, and they have an eye for the main chance. They can duck and weave when need be. The Scots tend to be rugged, disputatious, thrawn – individualists to the last.)

James, who was looking to the past rather than the future, absolutely refused to repudiate the Auld Alliance. His attitude to England remained dour and inconsistent.

Thus, when the canny and far-sighted Henry VII died, and was succeeded by Margaret's brother, the bombastic bellicose bully, Henry VIII, it was likely that there would be trouble. Soon the countries were at war, and just ten years after the marriage came Scotland's ultimate disaster, when James and more than 10,000 of his countrymen were killed at Flodden.

It took the Reformation, two generations later, to bring the two countries properly together again. In 1559, Scottish forces were trying unsuccessfully to drive the French, who had overstayed their welcome, out of our land. The new English queen, Elizabeth, sent both a fleet and an army to Scotland to help us. This aid had been energetically solicited by the dominant Scot of the day, the reformer John Knox, who admired the English and detested the French.

To send military aid to the Scots, Elizabeth had to breach her newly-signed treaty with the French. Many of her advisers counselled against helping us. The Archbishop of Canterbury, Matthew Parker, pointed out that Knox was a zealous egalitarian who wanted 'the *people* to be the orderers of things, God help us!' One of her generals even refused to lead an army to the aid of the Scots.

It would be, then, a brave gesture by the young English queen to defy the senior members of her court. But, after some hesitation, she did just that. She sent more than 10,000 troops north; and in 1560 the French were sent packing from Scotland, the English army returned to England cheered by grateful Scots, and, most importantly, the Scottish Reformation was secured.

A Scottish Parliament now assembled, ready to remould our nation. This was the most promising moment in our history, our one supreme political opportunity. But even now we evinced our calamitous tendency to self-destruct.

In his magnificent *First Book of Discipline*, the greatest political as well as religious document this nation has ever produced, Knox and five other Scots ministers had drawn up a radical blueprint that would have given Scotland the world's most advanced education system, based on equality of opportunity;

*In memory of
Flodden, The
Borders, 1952.*

*Glen Lyon,
Perthshire, 1981.*

introduced a national structure for the relief of poverty and made Scotland a dynamic, egalitarian, forward-looking country, at last able to harness its vast intellectual potential for its own ends rather than other people's. But it was far too revolutionary for the Scots Parliament, who rejected it.

Such craven incompetence by home-based Scots is all too typical. It is too easy to sit back and sneer at the Scots who leave, the John Buchans. The Scots who stay at home are often the worst culprits.

A similar fiasco to that of 1560 came as recently as 1979, in the referendum which should have granted the Scots a considerable measure of devolution from the English-dominated British Parliament. To be fair to the English, they devoted an enormous amount of parliamentary time in the 1970s to the preparation of the Scotland Bill, which eventually became law as the Scotland Act. But there was one flaw; it had to be endorsed by at least 40 per cent of the Scottish voters in a referendum.

This notorious '40 per cent' rule was championed not by an Englishman but by a redoubtable Scottish Labour MP who represented a North London seat – George Cunningham. For a time he was the most reviled man in Scotland. In the event, the Scots voted, by the narrowest of margins, for devolution – but came nowhere near passing the 40 per cent test. In fact the split was almost even: one-third voted for, one-third voted against, one-third abstained.

The referendum was preceded by a maelstrom of debate, much of it venomous and embittered. Another Scottish Labour MP, Tam Dalyell, in one of the classic expositions of what is now known as 'inferiorism', presented Scottish history prior to the Union as 'a gloomy, violent tale of murders and tribal revenge'. The Union with the English, however, had brought enlightenment and civilisation.

In the 11 years since the ill-fated referendum, the great Scottish-English debate has resumed its stagnant mode. Recently it has been marginally fired by football. (I was at Wembley twice in the 1970s; for reasons I won't go into here I fell asleep during the 5-1 debacle in 1975, but I stayed awake during the great 2-1 win in 1977. That was a marvellous night of celebration in London: I spent it in the company of a well-known Scottish MP who brandished his cherished piece of the Wembley turf round the West End. More recently I was one of those who infuriated my good friend and colleague Jack Webster by rooting for West Germany in their tight World Cup semi-final with England. I watched the game in Martinique, of all places; but even that exotic setting did not diminish my sheer tribal delight in England's defeat.)

I have a genuine respect and affection for the English. Why then should I, and many others like me, so enjoy it when they receive their sporting come-uppance? I turned for elucidation to Paul Scott, one of the most interesting men now living in Scotland, and somebody who should be much better known in our country, bereft as it for the most part is of significant personalities.

Paul is a distinguished former diplomat who is now rector of Dundee University, and one of the few genuine intellectuals in the SNP. He has written important books on the Act of Union and on Sir Walter Scott, and a pamphlet with the intriguing title of 'In Bed With An Elephant'. (The phrase was used by Pierre Trudeau to describe Canada's relationship with the US. Needless to say, Paul believes it applies to Scotland's relationship with England.)

'Well, I think the English are like the Germans,' he said. 'They can be civilised, charming, and they are a remarkable people. But they can also be ruthless and brutal. And frankly it is not possible to have a civilised relationship with people who constantly bugger you about. One of the main reasons for an independent Scotland is that it would at last allow us to have a civilised relationship with England.'

When I spoke to Paul he had just returned from a holiday on the Loire with a party of English. 'Those from the North of England were quite different from those from the South. The ones from the South were arrogant, braying, ignorant. They assumed Scotland was just a small and uninteresting part of Northern England.'

The Northern English, on the whole, do have a greater affinity with the Scots (though they tended to be much more virulent in their opposition to the devolution proposals of 1979 – perhaps because nothing similar was on offer for them).

We must always remember that England is a country of quite staggering diversity. That it has managed to maintain itself, let alone the UK, as a unitary state for so long is something of a political miracle. I have stayed for any length of time in only two English cities: Oxford (for three years) and Newcastle upon Tyne (for nine months). Two more utterly different cities it would be hard to imagine.

Again, my wife and I have been seeing in the New Year (one time when it is certainly advisable to escape from Scotland to England) for over a decade in the Fens, on the border of Norfolk and Cambridgeshire. There, with our English friends in those peculiar, atmospheric flatlands, I feel a million miles from London, let alone Glasgow or Edinburgh.

Indeed, part of our problem *vis-à-vis* the English is that their capital, their centre of power, is so far south. (If Scotland ever does gain independence, I sincerely hope that our capital will not be Edinburgh, but somewhere more central and suitable – perhaps Perth.) London's situation in the South-East can give otherwise educated Englishmen a quite ludicrous geographical perspective. (Hugo Young, in his acclaimed biography of Margaret Thatcher, describes Grantham as being in the North. The North, for goodness sake! As one who has travelled by train more times than I care to remember from King's Cross to Aberdeen, the thought of Grantham being in the 'North' is rancidly absurd.)

Until we Scots can develop some meaningful political expression of our nationhood, we are clearly going to be ill at ease with our English neighbours. Until that happy day, I think the best attitude to England is to regard it as a fertile and happy adjunct; a bonus, a pleasant place to visit, if not to stay. As I noted earlier, it seems an ideal place to celebrate New Year, for a start. There are times when being Scottish can be a pain.

Then take London. Last year in a special series for the *Herald* I investigated its growing squalor, its congestion, its tensions and disparities. It is undoubtedly becoming, for many of its citizens, an out-of-control mega-city, a hellish place in which to live and work.

But for the visitor, it can be uniquely rewarding. The Hungarian novelist Stephen Vizinczey believes that, despite everything, it is still the most civilised of the world's great cities. We Scots can enjoy what is has to offer – a great deal – without having to endure the stress and strain of actually living in it, or commuting to it every day. Yet perhaps the real England, as I have hinted above, is nothing to do with London. London is a huge international city which happens to be the centre of English power. (The young Scottish historian Graham Walker seriously believes that London is no longer an English city – in that its cultural and sociological links with the rest of England are becoming increasingly tenuous. But this is a problem for the English, not the Scots.)

Indeed I think the English, with their great imperial history, are going to find it harder and harder to come to terms with their lesser role in the world. They are already bad Europeans. (I have some sympathy for them in this. The good Europeans seem to be the ones who start the world wars.) But they are also going to find it harder and harder to define themselves, to canalise their nationalism meaningfully and constructively.

That is not going to be a problem for us: for too long we have not been allowed – and yes, we have not allowed ourselves – to be a real nation. Nationhood is ahead of us, not behind us. In that respect our future is much brighter and more full of hope than that of the English. Indeed, increasingly I feel that it is easier, despite our contrariness and argumentativeness, for a Scot to love Scotland than it is for an Englishman to love England.

I mentioned that in the summer I was in the Caribbean. Later in July I had two days in Glen Lyon, that loveliest of Scottish glens, in the very heart of our country, 30 glorious miles snaking up from the douce community of Fortingall where Pontius Pilate was reputedly born and where the kirk's yew tree is 3,000 years old (the oldest vegetation in Europe), probing up and up to the very heartland of Scotland, amid the splendid cathedrals which are the high tops of Breadalbane.

The second day we were climbing Stuchd an Lochain, one of the lesser-known Munros, but a distinguished mountain nonetheless. We climbed steadily in mist until, as we reached the broad plateau beneath the summit, the clouds cleared as if by magic. Immediately to the north – a great corrie and within it the perfect little circle of Lochan nan Cat, beyond that the lonely stretch of Loch an Daimh, and beyond that the great wilderness of Rannoch; to the west and the south – high peak after high peak; and down to the east, now glowing in sunlight – the long and glistening glen, a gleaming green mirage of natural woodland and gentle pasture. It was an epiphany.

As the referendum vote became history the advertising slogans changed, Glasgow, 1979.

For this, I thought, with unashamed sentimentality, is my country, and these are my hills. Do the English ever feel like this? Can they, these days, nurture such thoughts about *their* green and pleasant land? And can it compare, at all, with a landscape of such power and subtlety and grace and explosive magnificence as this? For this, this is mine, this is my . . . my Scotland.

Such moments never last too long. (Bathos is something the Scots, unlike the English, soon become hardened to.) Before long I was thinking again about the contradictions of being British, and about the strange two-way pull we Scots must endure.

I started by quoting John Buchan; let me finish by quoting a passage from another 20th-century Scottish writer, Lewis Grassic Gibbon, whom Jack McLean and John Linklater both write about elsewhere in this book. Gibbon, like Buchan, spent his mature life outside Scotland; much of it in Welwyn Garden City, of all places. Gibbon is less popular, but he is the better writer, and in this passage he expresses perfectly the old, old tension that all of us Scots have to resolve:

So that was Chris and her reading and schooling; two Chrisses there were that fought for her heart and tormented her. You hated the land and the coarse speak of the folk and learning was brave and fine one day and the next you'd waken with the peewits crying across the hills, deep and deep, crying in the heart of you and the smell of the earth in your face, almost you'd cry for that, the beauty of it and the sweetness of the Scottish land and skies. You saw their faces in firelight, father's and mother's and the neighbours', before the lamps lit up, tired and kind, faces dear and close to you, you wanted the words they'd known and used, forgotten in the far-off youngness of their lives, Scots words to tell to your heart, how they wrung it and held it, the toil of their days and unendingly their fight. And the next minute that passed from you, you were English, back to the English words so sharp and clean and true – for a while, for a while, till they slid so smooth from your throat you knew they could never say anything that was worth the saying at all.

England may be sweet but Scotland is sweeter.

ANNE SIMPSON

Thistle and Shamrock

Scotland and Ireland

TODAY THERE IS A FORCE NINE TEARING IN FROM THE ATLANTIC, STRAFING the squat stone cottages along the coast and hammering others even further down into the brackish hills. Johnny Coyne's grandparents would have recognised this unforgiving weather. More than a century ago it drove them to Port Glasgow from a tiny Galway cabin, and in its way that journey was as monumental as any planned for the opposite direction and the brazen promise of America.

Like those before them and ever since Johnny's people called this powerful empty landscape home and found it inhospitable. Little has changed yet everything has changed. Grandsires emigrate and return, emigrate and return, locked in a cycle of hope and regret. But today they can afford to travel back for weddings as well as funerals and the houses they re-enter are not so different from those that they leave elsewhere – bungalows of nondescript modernity with a trans-continental surplus of TV channels, and festoon drapes. In Mullaghglass, however, there will also be that timeless reminder of location; a mound of turf beehived tightly against the storms, and secured by nets anchored to the ground by Connemara rocks.

Wrapped around his seasonal versatility as harvester and brickie, Johnny Coyne's father was a folk-teller, the son himself a traditional fiddle player, and wherever their descendants settle now – Glasgow, Falkirk, Kilburn, Dundee or back again in Mullaghglass – these gifts follow to be demonstrated by the same impromptu verve which has always made a clatter of Coynes worth hearing. During mid-Victorian times, Scottish resentment against the Irish festered, but it is perhaps a testament to Scotland's later tolerance, as much as to the Coynes' conviviality, that this family would always return to Connemara voicing praise and affection for the decent, good-humoured Scots they worked beside in Port Glasgow.

Occasionally their fables astonished their own more rooted people raised on other stories of the Irish immigrant poor being ridiculed and discriminated against in the cruellest and most uncomprehending manner. In *A Century of the Scottish People 1830–1950*, the distinguished historian T. C. Smout observes that it is debatable to what extent the strength of Irish immigration into Scotland during the 1840s exacerbated divisions within the Scottish working class and aligned 'the respectable skilled workers still more firmly with the middle classes as they drew their skirts aside from the world of alien and unskilled Paddy'.

Yet, despite the miserable beginnings, there is hardly a Glaswegian or Dundonian of Irish descent who today – three generations on – doesn't proudly proclaim he is Scottish by nature, Irish by sentiment. And for those relatives remaining in Donegal there is a preference for looking to Glasgow as their capital city rather than Dublin. This sense of settled identity, this absorption into the social fabric of Scottish life, must, according to Smout, be recognised as one of the major achievements of Scottish history. At first the Irish 'were distrusted, despised, treated as inherently comic, drunken and

Dr Michael Kelly practises the bagpipes in Glasgow's City Chambers, 1983.

THISTLE
AND
SHAMROCK

The Apprentice Boys' March in Glasgow, 1989.

superstitious, and were the butt of Orangist attacks both in the coalfields and the cities'.

But while outraged respectability dismissed them as wastrels and 'a contaminating element in Scottish working life', the Irish themselves, as Smout records, were gradually integrating through membership of the trade unions although these initially had blamed them for 'coming over and taking Scottish jobs'. Beyond this political solidarity, with other working men, they further secured their identity by forming football clubs 'albeit often rivals to Protestant ones'.

These remained the chief participatory outlets until the 1950s and 1960s when a graduate generation, its origins in that same Irish émigré class, was poised to make the new inroad into Scottish professional and public life. Among that first substantial batch of lawyers, accountants, political scientists, historians and psychologists was Michael Kelly who intrepidly used his role of Lord Provost to pursue an international status for Glasgow as a city of tourism and hectic artistic adventure. At first the very notion, given Glasgow's entrenched dilapidation seemed preposterous, but inspired by the rejuvenation of New York in the 1970s, the Kelly campaign survived disbelief and derision as he and his team gradually managed to align Tory business interest with the Labour administration's policies.

Kelly's grandfather, James Kelly, played football for Renton, and captained Scotland in the 1880s. His great-grandfather had been included in the 1840 census in Alexandria, and although Michael had grown up in a home that respected these origins it was not one burdened with an awareness of bigotry or immigrant insecurities. Yet had he ever encountered any innuendo of prejudice during his tenure as Lord Provost?

From the headquarters of his public relations consultancy in Glasgow Michael Kelly reflects that he can't honestly recall ever suffering any discrimination. 'Maybe I'm just naïve, but I never went out looking for it, although I do know some Catholics would say that they have experienced prejudice against them in the past and that in some areas it probably still exists.'

Equally, though, the question arises of whether a Catholic mafia operates in the West of Scotland, and perhaps the most obvious answer in Glasgow lies in the Catholics' seeming monopoly on the Lord Provost role. 'I don't think that you could claim there is any such thing as a conspiracy because all Lords Provost are genuinely the electorate's choice,' says one observer. 'But in a council where the overwhelming majority are Catholic you do hear the phrase: "He's one of us", and that's not a reference to the said person's membership of the Labour Party or the fact that he lives in Pollockshields.'

If anything, the bias springs from the old, unrefined belief of any group with memories of under-privilege stowed somewhere in its baggage, that the only way to experience power is by indissoluble bonding. But just like the Masonry of the other side, the subject is a swampland of sensibilities, whose coded signals and irrational girnings are virtually incomprehensible to the outsider. Yet if discrimination, from either Catholics or Protestants, surfaces overtly today it does so exposing nothing so much as the red-neck insularity of its owners. Even so, until relatively recently, its talent for the primitive sneer was not unknown in some of the most allegedly genteel quarters.

Dr Elizabeth Wilson, who until her retirement was one of the pioneering family planning doctors in Scotland, remembers an occasion shortly after her arrival in Glasgow in the mid-1960s when she was confronted by a delegation of Kelvinside parents requesting that her young sons and their friends change the colour of their street football strip – because the choice of green, it was

Pope John Paul II and Professor John McIntyre, Moderator, pass the John Knox statue, Edinburgh, 1982.

felt, lowered the tone of the neighbourhood. 'As I am English I was just incredulous and that must have been an eye-opener to them. But gosh, we have come a long way since those days.'

On a more felicitous level the long way back to Donegal from Glasgow is still the preferred route for many people. For almost 20 years Danny Collins's fleet of coaches has been jaunting émigré Irish and the Scottish sightseer to Ireland via the ferries at Cairnryan and Stranraer. At first the service only operated in a modest way, depositing families, seasonal labourers, the occasional priest and maiden aunts no farther than Larne. From there, equipped with the unmanageable luggage of family holidays and the kind of homely misshapen parcels that always signify relatives at the other end, the travellers had to make their own way to Belfast and Derry and the wildest tracts of Donegal's Falcarragh and Gortahork.

But as demand increased, defying all Northern Ireland's headlines of atrocity, so the service extended to include other small coach hire businesses which operate right through the year with daily runs in July and August. By tradition the Gorbals is the principal pick-up point in Glasgow and even just after eight in the morning the mood is relaxed and jocular, with mothers squashing excited children into cramped old-fashioned seats, students abandoning futile attempts at negotiating rucksacks down the aisle and old bachelors, or maybe widowers, returning home, still with a glint in the eye. Continued service rather than the occupants' disrespect has reduced the seating to a pretty springless state, and to sit in it, as we did on and off for six hours, is to become so wedged in by upholstery that your very skin begins to take in the aroma of moquette. For between £20 and £26 per head most coaches operate a relay system, the first stage ending at the ferry, the second coming into play at Larne, and others collecting passengers for places like Strabane and Lifford at various feeder points along the route. Since the extent of any journey may depend on those who turn up in the first place the itinerary is often spontaneous. That said, by charabanc to Donegal is still one of life's genuine, if humble adventures, shuttling travellers between the urban cheekiness of Glasgow and the intimate, densely textured countryside towards Lough Swilley and Rathmullen. Today most Irish Scots feel themselves harmoniously at one in both places. If they really have a hero it is not likely to be some 'martyred' republican but Glasgow Celtic's Donegal goalkeeper Pat Bonner, a man whom they like to think of as their representative, striding easily in two lands.

At Dublin Airport the passengers for the early morning flights to Edinburgh and Glasgow, in contrast to Danny Collins's clientèle, are as formally suited as any on the London shuttle. Today the Irish executive commutes sometimes with weekly frequency to the smaller Scottish firms requiring specialist expertise in electronics. In the first instance they will have been introduced to the market by the Scottish office in Glasgow of Coras Trachtala, the Irish Export Board, whose own changing role in the past ten years reflects economic developments in both countries. In the early 1980s Coras Trachtala's main aim revolved around exploiting retail opportunities for Irish craft and fashion goods as well as foodstuffs like Kerrygold. Today it acts more as a sorting house for new industries, matching source with demand right from Ayrshire, through the central belt and up to Aberdeen.

Of course the decline of heavy industry and the secularisation of society have accelerated the process of integration enormously. Until 20 years ago it would have been difficult for Catholics to gain jobs with many of the major West of Scotland employers, including – it must be said – the

*Pope John Paul
II leaves St
Mary's Cathedral,
Edinburgh, 1982.*

Glasgow Herald. One senior manager tells the story of three piles of
job applications, as sifted by the personnel department. When he inquired
what they were he was informed that the first represented the possibles, the
second the rejects and the third: 'those you won't want to see', a euphemism
meaning that the applicants were Catholic. Nowadays with the erosion of
the masonic craft-unions and the arrival of new technology such ploys are
irrelevant, although it would be foolish to imagine that residual bigotry has
disappeared completely. Yet its social significance is of scant importance now
and is channelled almost exclusively through football clubs whose terraces
remain as tribally choral as ever but whose anthems are more knee-jerk
party pieces than any serious pledge of loyalty to Northern Ireland's reprisal
executioners.

Catholic insistence on separate schools might be claimed to perpetuate
social divisions, although the desire on the part of the Catholic community
lies not so much in bigotry as in the belief that educational separatism is
an inalienable right. But if Belfast has always presented the spectre of what
Glasgow might have become, much of the preventative credit must belong
to the Labour Party in the West of Scotland, which over generations has
determinedly unified the two groups of working class, and in the past ten
years especially, has functioned in Glasgow with entrepreneurial flourish. By
contrast, in Northern Ireland working-class Protestants and working-class
Catholics have been ruthlessly set at each others' throats by the forces of
opposing nationalism.

In the first week of June in 1982 something happened in Scotland which
ensured that Irish Scots would never feel defensive again. At the end of a
remarkable journey to Britain, Pope John Paul travelled North, crossing the
border into the heartland of history's darkest warnings against Rome. After
the momentum of Westminster and Canterbury, the merriment of Liverpool,
superlatives among the press corps were difficult to muster. Nevertheless
nothing could take from the fact that at Murrayfield in Edinburgh and in
Bellahouston Park in Glasgow the Scots decided to turn the visit into a giant
ceilidh. 'It could so easily have seemed like triumphalism', recalls one parish

priest. 'But the rest of Scotland also seemed quite genuinely happy and moved by the occasion. The Pope had relieved any sense of inferiority and without pomp the Catholics knew they had arrived.'

The Pope also left his Irish-Scottish flock with many reasons for reflection. His strict teachings on morals and sexuality brought little comfort to the liberal-minded, but it was the message that the conservative Scottish hierarchy particularly wanted to hear. They wished the Pope to affirm authority over a young, restless generation inclined to miss Mass, favour birth control, and accept divorce, and although there was no explicit warning against social permissiveness the call for spiritual and moral discipline could not be mistaken. In the electric, festive atmosphere, the words were greeted with ecstatic cheers but only the priests who hear confession know whether John Paul's teaching has had its intended effect.

But what the Pope specifically recognised was Scotland's special identity. He chose his words about the nation brilliantly, acknowledging the sense of isolation it has often felt 'situated on the remote edge of Europe' and thus he understood its loneliness and individualism and the valour of all its early crusading Christians. No one had expected or sought the moving symbolism of Canterbury's embrace, yet there is little doubt about the durable fellowship exchanged between the then Moderator of the General Assembly, Professor John McIntyre, and the pilgrim Pope, John Paul. In most countries of the Western world the ecumenical greetings of that June day would have been simply accepted as the standard courtesies of clergymen. But in the very shadow of John Knox such welcome, pleasure and mutual gratitude were quietly momentous. Two men had met with dignity and genuine respect and given history a brighter, more rewarding face.

JULIE DAVIDSON
Heederum-Hoderum
Scottish Kitsch

*Haggis 'n' kilts,
Glasgow, 1981.*

LAST YEAR I VISITED SIENA FOR THE FIRST TIME; ON A CALM NOVEMBER
Sunday when, for an hour or two in the morning, the Campo's great scallop of
herring-bone brickwork was almost empty. The tourist season had paused for
breath, but by the time I climbed to the cathedral the town was gently humming
with the sound of Italians enjoying their own sights. Siena Cathedral is an
extraordinary building: a candy-stripe confection of black-and-white marble
which takes its shape from the Gothic and its substance from the mosques of
Islam. It made me want to laugh.

And so did the Pinturicchio fresco in the cathedral's gorgeous library
which shows James I of Scotland holding an audience for the Siena-born
poet and diplomat Aeneas Sylvius Piccolomini, who became Pope Pius II.
This Philistine response to one of the glories of the Sienese school can be
explained, if not excused, by Pinturicchio's vision of Scotland, which he had
clearly not visited. As the king receives his Italian guest, elegant Renaissance
courtiers strike poses beneath classical marble pillars; in the background,
mountains, loch and castle are given their due but the mountains look like
the Tuscan hills and the loch is as limpid as Como and the castle is a fantasy.
It's the start of the 16th century and already Scotland is beginning to work
its way into the romantic imagination.

Is this fresco, I asked myself, the first exquisite step on the road that leads
to tartan madness? The kind of lunacy that ends in the souvenir shops of the
Royal Mile, where 'Gnomo Sapiens' – a crude clay mannikin in a kilt – is
defined as 'the Chieftain of the Tartan Gnomes and Lord High Protector
of the Haggis'? It may have taken nearly four centuries for high art to
find a resonance in low kitsch, but Bernardino Pinturicchio's land of the
mountain and the flood must be one of the earliest examples of Scotland
mythologised.

Who do we blame for the traducing of Scotland? For the fantasies
and falsehoods that have afflicted its history, culture, character and even
landscape in the 300-odd years since we lost our nationhood? A long line of
offenders has been cited: James Macpherson and his fake bard Ossian, whose
Fragments of Ancient Poetry caught the mood of the Romantic Movement
and brought Mendelssohn to Fingal's Cave; Robert Burns and his tenacious
celebration of the dram; Sir Walter Scott and his 'marketing' of the Gael,
particularly to the English establishment ('The Highlanders are what he will
most like to see,' he opined in advance of George IV's visit to Edinburgh);
Queen Victoria and Balmorality; Harry Lauder, who successfully exported a
grotesque caricature of Scottishness; Hollywood, which processed Scotland
through its stupendous myth-making machine in Brigadoon; and, today, the
Scottish Tourist Board.

It's all such a worry to us. At least, it's a worry to those who believe that
the 'Scotch Myths' identified by Murray and Barbara Grigor in their seminal
exhibition at the Edinburgh International Festival in 1981 have given us a
tartan ghost of nationhood to compensate for the real thing. It's also a
worry to those who worry about the tourists and what they think of us,

but to my mind that's one worry too many. There may be some peculiarly self-denigrating aspects to the great tartan monster which the Scottish tourist industry exploits, but other countries have its counterpart – and dirndls and lederhosen and oom-pa-pa bands playing in pretty Tirolean villages don't make us forget that Hitler was an Austrian.

No. The real anxiety about Scotland's kitsch industry – the whole heederum-hoderum, heuchter-teuchter, dram-and-shortie subculture which affects to derive from the grim and feudal social system of the clans – is what it does to us, rather than the tourists. As far as Scotland is concerned tourism is, depending on your point of view, either a lost cause or a successful and secure one. The industry is now officially the country's most important, sustaining 180,000 full-time jobs and generating £18 million a year.

It's valuable. No one questions that. What should be questioned, however, are its values – its impact on our heartachingly lovely landscape and the methods it uses to peddle an inadequate and sometimes warped version of Scottish history and Scottish culture. In the year when the European Community has designated the whole country a 'theme park' the chairman of the Scottish Tourist Board describes Scotland as a 'quality product', and exhorts area tourist boards to promote their local attractions and extend the season round the year.

We can expect to see even more road signs disfiguring the landscape, labelling scenic routes and 'tourist trails', pointing the way to visitor centres and 'living' museums which filter all the anguish, passion and complexity of Scotland's past through the painless entertainment of multi-media 'experiences' and dressed-up locals fiddling with spinning wheels and claymores. What does this do for the native Scot, never mind the visitor? It serves us up our own history in oversimplified, easily digested, portion-controlled helpings, removing the incentive to read, question, assess and speculate for ourselves. Look what knee-jerk history has done for John Knox, the nation's totem to bigotry, joylessness and oppression. How many Scots know that this egalitarian revolutionary's ideas were unique in Europe and laid the groundwork for universal education – or that he called for two hogsheads of wine when he was dying so that his friends could hold a rousing wake?

Meanwhile, even Scotland's place names get nibbled away in order to explain themselves to strangers. As you enter Strathspey – and the Scottish word for valley is as benign and comely as the place itself – you are told that you are entering the Spey Valley. In another generation we will have lost the word 'strath'.

The great tourist nations of mainland Europe, Switzerland, Spain, Italy France and Greece, have their own examples of cultural and historical affronts and their own grisly souvenir industries. The town of Sorrento is kitted out with a kind of civic musak, piping Neapolitan songs into its streets, and I've seen seashell Parthenons in Athens and General de Gaulle ballpoints in Paris. But for all their own rich histories they haven't constructed a heritage industry in quite the same organised, 'presentational' way as we've done.

England, if anything, is even more afflicted with heritage fever than Scotland. Its motorways are littered with big brown signposts advertising everything from Old Mother Shipton's Cave (an undistinguished hole in Yorkshire reputed to have been the den of a soothsayer) to Captain Cook Country (a corner of Cleveland where the antipodean adventurer was merely born). I remain astonished and grateful that the plain, dignified village of Lumphanan in Aberdeenshire hasn't so crudely exploited its associations

Sir Harry Lauder
advises Churchill,
Edinburgh,
1946.

*Sir Harry Lauder on
a caravan trip, Loch
Lomond, 1936.*

with Macbeth. It's claimed that the doomed king fought his last battle at Lumphanan, where Macbeth's Cairn is alleged to mark his grave (in fact, like many early Scottish kings, he's buried on Iona) but at the time of writing there is no big brown signpost advertising Macbeth Country.

The bureaucrats and entrepreneurs of the tourist industry will argue that Britain's fickle climate demands this beefing-up of the attractions of our antiquities, whereas the Roman Forum, the Alhambra in Granada and the entire city of Venice can get by on sunshine. But it's my belief that England's especially enthusiastic espousal of American-style heritage 'concepts' (conceived by a nation whose short history required some promotion and which took its cue from the ingenious theme parks of Walt Disney) also has something to do with a crisis of identity similar to that which seized Scotland after the Act of Union in 1707.

England more than Scotland, which lost its sovereignty nearly 300 years ago, fears the growing hegemony of the European Community. England doesn't want to surrender the Mother of Parliaments to the legislative will of a European federation. England is also still struggling to come to terms with the loss of empire and a piecemeal retreat from the centre of the world stage. It's a theory of mine that the dread of further loss and the threat to all the old sustaining English totems – oldest continuous democracy in the world, land of hope and glory, Hitler's bane, this sceptred isle, uninvaded since 1066 – are at the root of the epidemic of heritage centres. Who are they for? The English more than the tourists, as England revisits a more heroic and visionary past.

Something similar went on in Scotland in the 18th century, although Scotland had fewer glories to draw upon, other than its Wars of Independence and a less glorious series of internecine struggles. (The wounds of the religious conflicts which followed the Reformation were still too raw for that event to be celebrated.) Ever inventive, however, the Scots began to make up a few fictions. Murray Grigor has argued that the Scottish national identity crisis followed the destruction of the clan system after the '45, but as most of Lowland Scotland was delighted to encourage the dismantling of these tribes and the disenfranchising of their quarrelsome chiefs this is only part of the story.

What is clear, however, is that the alternative culture of the Gael, once his teeth were drawn, and the splendour of his environment were the stuff of which myths are made, and the fraudulent work of a trainee Church of Scotland minister and putative Gaelic scholar was a primary source of Celtic Romanticism.

If the aftermath of the '45 was only one stimulant to the quest to recover our national identity, it did coincide with a growing need in Europe for a northern alternative to classicism. Murray Grigor writes: 'The time was ripe for a great romantic hero and Ossian was born to fill the bill.' When, in 1760, James Macpherson published his alleged translations of the poetry of the third-century bard, at a stroke he 'dealt Scotland a glorious and heroic past (albeit an Irish Celtic one) and a place in the vanguard of European thought bent on creating the Romantic Movement'.

Macpherson's literary thunderbolt has left a legacy of 122 separate editions and translations indexed under Ossian in the National Library of Scotland. Ossianism held the Continent in its thrall for the next 50 years, influencing a generation of painters like Ingres and writers like Goethe. Later, Napoleon took him on board ('I have been even accused of having my head filled with Ossian's clouds') and although Anglo-Scottish interest centred on whether or not the works were authentic the imprint of Ossian's Celtic otherworld –

A corner of the curio room, Lauder Ha', 1966.

*A Frenchman shows
his friend how the
pipes should be held,
1951.*

a majestic, melancholy landscape peopled by simple but poetic Highlanders – almost certainly helped create the climate which made Europe so receptive to the fiction of Sir Walter Scott.

Scott's role in the myth-making industry is one of the running battle-grounds of Scottish intellectual life. He has been accused, albeit at a nobler level than Macpherson, of romanticising the Highlands and the Gael as well as his own Borders and Borderers, and there's no doubt that he was the architect of an early tourist industry. Washington Irvine in his account *Abbotsford* records his disappointment with his first sight of the Borders – 'a mere succession of grey waving hills . . . monotonous in their aspect and destitute of trees . . . and yet such had been the magic web of poetry and romance thrown over the whole that it had a greater charm for me than the richest scenery I beheld in England'.

When Irvine charged Scott with encouraging an 'influx of curious travellers' through the romantic associations of his work the writer 'laughed and said I might in some measure be right and recollected a circumstance in point. He recalled an old woman who kept an inn at Glenross who recognised him as the gentleman who had written a bonnie book about Loch Katrine. She begged him to write a little book about their lake, too, for she understood his book had done the inn at Loch Katrine a muckle deal of good.'

If it seems grudging that we now complain of Scott's promotion of the 'quality product' then not everyone does. The writer Allan Massie, a zealous admirer, believes that far from falsifying our history the Wizard of the North 'fired the imagination of Europe and restored Scotland's consciousness of itself as an historic nation'. And he finds the value of the novelist's understanding of Scotland incalculable: 'The more of Scott's works you read, the more you read about Scott, the more you find yourself saying "Why, this is Scotland; if I come really to know Scott I shall know all that is best and strangest about my country".' Massie also makes a virtue out of the contradictions in Scott's character, explaining them as part of the quintessentially Scottish temperament, and answers the charge that he 'toadied' to the English establishment with a celebration of ambivalence: 'He was a fervent Scottish patriot, jealous of any encroachment on the liberties of his country; no man did more to feed national pride, and yet no man did more to reconcile Scots to the Union with England.'

And, indeed, to reconcile the English to a palatable version of Scotland. As the stage manager of George IV's visit to Edinburgh in 1822 he launched an event which was to turn the once-proscribed dress of the Highlander into an international symbol of Scotland. If any single person sowed the seed which spawned the great tartan monster it was Sir Walter Scott. It must have been a bitter-sweet moment for the rehabilitated clan chiefs when they were summoned to the city with selected clansmen 'of decided respectability, dress and accoutrements to be in order', and found their monarch swathed in Highland regalia from head to foot.

The weavers had invented a tartan for the king, soon to be called the Royal Stewart, and from then on anyone with the money to commission their own tartan would find no lack of willing designers. The great tartan monster had taken its first steps on a rampage which was to cross the world, from Highland Games in Wellington, New Zealand, to citrus orchards in Tulare Country, California, where the descendants of Scots immigrant communities pack oranges in tartan boxes and give them names like Loch Lomond, Bonnie Lassie Jean and Highland Maid.

It quickly became clear (most spectacularly in the growing Scotch whisky industry) that the great tartan monster was no marketing man's nightmare.

And Micheil Macdonald, curator (and creator) of the award-winning Highland Tryst Museum in Crieff, finds some redeeming aspects in its kaleidoscopic features. He writes: 'Many of the trappings of our Scottishness, partly because of Scott's romanticism, charged a Highland population of dynamic apathy into a new spirit and pride in itself. At the same time it bred in many who weren't Highlanders the need for acceptance of a kind of tartanocracy of the early nineteenth century.'

As the century advanced, however, and Queen Victoria maintained the Royal patronage of the Highlands with the building of Balmoral, inspiring a rash of minor-imitations in shooting lodges and Big Houses, most of them owned by English industrialists whose vision of Scotland coincided with that of the painter Landseer, the monster began to pick up bad habits. The poetry of Robert Burns, however finely turned and however popularly judged, had presented the world with a new and persistent Scottish stereotype: the drunk. The bibulous Scotsman, now also associated with obsessive thrift, began to be caricatured in the cartoons of *Punch* and, around the turn of the century, in a vigorous picture postcard industry.

Edinburgh was a centre of that industry. In fact, George Stewart of Edinburgh is credited with inventing the first British picture postcard in 1895, and W. and A. K. Johnston of Edinburgh and London produced a celebrated series of cards comically illustrating quotes from Burns. Scotsmen takin' aff their drams featured heavily. 'Under the inspiring tutelage of the National Bard, Scotland has become one of the drunkenest nations in the world,' wrote T. W. H. Crosland in a provocative anti-Scottish tract. But Scots themselves were conspiring in the manufacture of the caricature and profiting by it.

By the time Harry Lauder arrived on Broadway, gnarled crummock in one hand and wee doch-an-doris in the other, the image was fixed: the archetypal Scot was pawky, tight-fisted, crapulent, sentimental and aggressive – not to mention agonisingly arch about what he wore under his kilt. And the kilt itself? 'In the music hall,' writes one critic, Brian Dunnigan, 'the tartan of Walter Scottland and Balmorality is still in evidence but transferred from red-haired giants to knock-kneed dwarfs . . .'

Both representatives of the race – the romantic tribes of Ossian and Sir Walter and the comic heirs of Burns and Harry Lauder – have since been processed through the dream factory of Hollywood in films like *Bonnie Prince Charlie*, *Rob Roy*, *Whisky Galore* and *The Maggie* and – the apotheosis – *Brigadoon*, in which all the stock elements of fantasy Scotland were brought together by two New York Jews and an American Italian (the composers Lerner and Loewe and the film director Vincent Minelli). The Highland village of Brigadoon, a symbol of simple values, rural virtues and enduring love, is a fairy tale village: it only appears to mortal eyes every 100 years, which is rather more often than the weird Scotland it represents.

In the 1960s television took up many of the same themes, most notably in our own back yard. But after years of *White Heather Clubs* and *Thingummyjigs* and Hogmanay hooleys, the studios of STV and BBC Scotland now find themselves in a cultural vacuum on New Year's Eve. Shamed into wiping their screens clean of tartan and haggis by that body of intellectual opinion (but not popular opinion) which saw degradation in these up-yer-kilt productions, they have still not managed to find a Hogmanay celebration which satisfies Scotland.

The fact is that for most Scots the myths have taken on reality. We share an inherited nostalgia for a land that never was. It isn't only ex-pats whose eyes grow misty when Moira Anderson sings 'My Ain Folk'; and when the

Touring Scotland, Forth Rail Bridge, 1951.

James Adam paid £180 for this Sir Harry Lauder Jug at Christie's Edmiston's sale, 1983.

HEEDERUM-
HODERUM

*Three pipers in
repose at Dunsapie
Loch, Holyrood
Park, Edinburgh,
1958.*

*The Lothian and
Borders Police
Pipe Band pass the
Royal Scots Greys
War Memorial,
Edinburgh, 1975.*

*Laurel and Hardy,
Edinburgh.*

pipes play 'Scotland the Brave' or the Corries sing 'Flower of Scotland', from Shotts to Stornoway, from Kilmarnock to Kirkwall and Portobello to Portree the hairs rise on the backs of five million necks. The great tartan monster has become our national mascot. It's even possible to argue that this bizarre beastie has played its part in reinforcing that sense of identity which might so easily have vanished after the Act of Union.

True, the symbol of that identity may be a peculiar mongrel mix of marketing emblems and kailyard stereotypes and historical distortions, and it may repel some Scots. But like it or loathe it, it's become our corporate logo. We can't uninvent it. But at least we can try to make sure we understand the elements which went into its design.

WILLIAM HUNTER

Bumptious and Impident (Eh?)
The Global Scot

IT IS A TRUTH UNIVERSALLY ACKNOWLEDGED THAT THE SCOTCH population of the world numbers 20 million. Three times as many Jocks play away as at home. Everybody says so. Whether so wide a spread of tartan means strength or shame is less certain. Never, however, is there a quarrel about the count. Twenty millions sound about right and may be so. But it was a statistic pulled out of the air. Somebody looked into a saltire-blue sky and saw 20,000,000 etched in fluffy clouds. He was Thomas Johnston, mightiest of Secretaries of State for Scotland, who, among many other hats he later put on, became in 1949 the first chairman of the Scottish Tourist Board. Now reckoned to be the premier industry, heaven help us all, tourism was then rated seventh in size, although it might have been sixth. (Tom Johnston was a newspaperman by trade, as was his closest aide on the board, and arithmetic is not the most reliable of journalistic skills.) As the new impresario of the holiday trade he preached three missions: to extend the season to include May and October; see to the slaughter of the Highland midge; and encourage all the Scots of the diaspora overseas (an expression he loved to utter) to come back for their hols. His propaganda guess of 20 million became a tablet handed down from the highest ben. In his speeches he kept chiselling the total afresh. Verily, it endureth.

Scotch cheek includes a wish to be seen as multitudinous. Whence comes the lasting popularity of Mr Johnston's creative arithmetic. An endearing piece of effrontery is to glory in being a small country that is not small at all. From a fancy for wider frontiers arises also much enthusiasm for nostalgia. Yesterday's heroes are not allowed to die. Names of antique inventors and mighty swordsmen of yore are recited as if still at work or war. Their presence sustains the idea of a greater land. Even the weather helps the illusion and so does the terrain. When one day's journey can pass through wild changes of scenery and through most of the elements of the four seasons, a traveller's joy is to feel he is on safari through a landscape that is vast. This little-bigness of the territory is a portion of the trauchle of being Scotch. Droogled with earnest ink in the public prints, it gets called the crisis of national identity. What crisis? Some crisis, if 20 million share it!

When in my second deepest mood of oatcake gloom (saving the most morose until the end), it can feel that the hardest place to be Scotch is in Scotland. Here you can get by with being a little English-hater, who sleeps in his kilt to be aye ready to get tore into the Saxons. Those of the diaspora overseas enjoy a fuller horizon. Their pleasure is to assert what they hold to be traditional Scotch traits and to admire traditional Scotch virtues. Canniness, hardiness, good thrift, ambitiousness, and fighting pride are a diet of thin porridge to the stay-at-homes in the garret above the Cheviots. It can be a comic-cuts country. To support their idea of themselves the aborigines use both belt and braces. Two flags are waved, two languages spoken, two sporting anthems sung. Political life is scripted by those twin handbooks of philosophy, the *Dandy* and the *Beano*.

Whether or not frontier-less, nationality is a big problem, it is a small

Tom Johnston, later to become Secretary of State, at Norwood, 1924.

*Scottish Tourist
Board Poster
Competition,
Edinburgh,
1949.*

*Highland Games,
Antigonish, Nova
Scotia, 1983.*

pest. Even signing an hotel register becomes an ethnic anguish when a nosey innkeeper expects a declaration about which tribe I belong to. Will he insist on Brit to let me in? (I ask myself). What will suit his book? It is an absurd quandary like the little old lady's when confronted on an official form with the box marked Sex. After honest introspection she put *Seldom*. Against nationality for better purposes than hotel registration, perhaps, and to be honest, I should declare *Now and again*.

Once upon a time (or in 1966) coal miners made a grand march on the House of Commons. To Westminster from all of its areas the National Union of Mineworkers had organised an angry pilgrimage. Scotland's squad of 400, who had flown from Renfrew and Turnhouse with pipe bands, gave the uprising its swagger. When it came to parading, the Scotch contingent were cocks o' the North. They had the best tunes, the proudest banners, the most gusto, the liveliest humour. Yet how the long day stays in the mind is for its sadness and lostness. Some Ayrshire men, able to work in 18-inch seams, couldn't find their way through pedestrian subways at Marble Arch for a cup of tea. Later around St James Street, a raw Fife boy accosted a local toff at the portals of his club. The English gent was almost a caricature of metropolitan elegance, his brolly severely rolled as a mob stick. He was affably polite. If the miner's rough intensity struck him like a fist, he didn't blink. On both sides there were good manners. But the passion was all one-way. About the encounter there was no communication. They spoke different languages. Where they met was out of sight of where men dig for coal, but they might have come from opposite ends of the earth. When the marchers had put on their kitchen lights that morning in the pit-village houses, it had been pitch black outside. When they first felt the sun, it was blasting off the high white walls of Park Lane. It was a two-nation meeting with a vengeance. Intending to assault a citadel, the miners were treated as tourists. On the retreat home they shook their heads, baffled. Agreeing that even by NUM standards their demands were utopian (guaranteed new jobs for old ones), they thought they could have handled hard common sense and hostility. What had unmanned them was amiable indifference.

London now has lost much of its distant enchantment. It is less faraway and not awesome at all. Perversely, however, the Celts keep insisting that being different from the Saxons is paramount. Oliver Brown, schoolteacher and patriot, liked to say that when he met an old Etonian he came to the conclusion that the Scots were complete barbarians. 'When I meet two of them, I thank God for it,' he added. Even while Jock knows right down to his woolly socks that he belongs to a world tribe of 20 million, he persists in feeling beleaguered. For his part, Tom Johnstone accepted the consequences of his own imaginative counting of heads. In his *Memories* (published in 1952) he wrote:

> What can they know of Scotland who only Scotland know? The greater Scotland beyond the seas with its nostalgia for the old birth-place is a fact of some importance in the world, and who having experienced it, can ever forget the overpowering intensity of the Scottishness in the gatherings of our folk from Calcutta to Chicago? The singing of the *Road to the Isles*, *Hail Caledonia*, *Scots Wha Hae*, the *Bonnie Banks of Loch Lomond*, and the *Tammie Wi' the Wee Toorie on It*.

Such Wha Haeism has some home Macs reaching for their dirks. Attempts to stir sentimental salt into their porridge is asking for a fight. Queasiness results from what James Bridie, a family doctor and playwright, decried as the slop of Wallacethebrucism and mayainfolkism. They seem not to be diseases which carry. Emigré Scots, who have skedaddled from the croft and prospered, know how to wrap themselves in tartan without suffocating in it. Stuck at home, their ain folk turn on each other. Neebors fecht in momentously tiny quarrels. Haggis is made a bone of contention. Otherwise sensible people get in a tizzy about the use of the word Scotch, except in connection with comestibles. Burns suppers are tucked into as one of the loveliest nights of the year when they are not sneered at as orgies of illiteracy. Well-travelled Donalds and Bellas, who know that the world's phone books are flamboyant with Mac entries, reject as parochial any wee scene that depicts the home country as a land o' the heather and the kilt. Here is the curse of the thistle. It is this mixture of the practical and the emotional that makes Scotchness such a slippery fish to grasp. Still and all, there has never been any reluctance to leave Scotchness well alone.

Auld Scotia's strength can most clearly be seen in the quality of some old enemies. While the most robust foes have conceded that 'Made in Scotland' remains in the world's eye a label of quality, whether of whisky or salmon or a magical knack for machinery, even more reassuring has been the quality of their abuse. Seldom has any small country aroused such warmth as Samuel Johnson, say, exuded. Even the genial P. G. Wodehouse, novelist and lyricist, felt moved to add his quota: 'It is never difficult [he quoth] to distinguish between a Scotsman with a grievance and a ray of sunshine.' Gentle Charles Lamb, essayist and office clerk, was constrained to utter: 'The tediousness of these people is certainly provoking. I wonder if they ever tire one another!' We are not even allowed to suffer our weather in peace. Sydney Smith, preacher and wag, took the trouble to write: 'They would have you even believe they can ripen fruit; and to be candid, I must own in remarkably warm summers I have tasted peaches that made most excellent pickles . . .'

Always the tribe's oft-expressed wish to see themselves as others see them has been amply rewarded, nowhere more so than in a forgotten diatribe called *The Unspeakable Scot* (1902). Here is a short sour taste:

> Your proper child of Caledonia believes in his rickety bones that he is the salt of the earth. Prompted by a glazing pride, not to say by a black and consuming avarice, he has proclaimed his saltiness from the house-tops in and out of season, unblushingly, assiduously, and with results which have no doubt been most satisfactory from his own point of view. There is nothing creditable to the race of men, from filial piety to a pretty taste in claret, which he has not sedulously advertised as a virtue peculiar to himself. This arrogation has served him passing well. It has brought him into unrivalled esteem. He is one species of human animal that is taken by all the world to be fifty per cent cleverer and pluckier and honester than the facts warrant. He is the daw with a peacock's tail of his own painting. He is the ass who has been at pains to cultivate the convincing roar of a lion. He is the fine gentleman whose father toils with a muck-fork.

Such good abuse, with plenty more, was a giftie from T. W. H. Crosland, poet and journalist. For so wide a scatter of insult there was limited cause. What stuck up Will Crosland's Yorkshire nose was the excessive influence in London of Scotch writers. He thought they had as much true imagination as a hat box. Crosland's dislike had a different starting point from Lamb's. While Lamb said he had tried to like Scotchmen only to give up in despair, Crosland claimed he felt contempt. Charlie Lamb wearied of the firmness with which we express obvious truths; Wullie Crosland would not even allow us our dourness. He insisted it was only a condition of constant hangover from crudest whisky. When his book, a bestseller, reached Scotland, it was

A 50-ton steel casting made at Beardmore's Parkhead Forge, Glasgow, 1938.

Sculpture at Parkhead Forge, Glasgow, 1988.

The Toast to the Haggis, British Legion Burns Supper, Trades House, Glasgow, 1938.

smiled upon. 'Highly diverting,' opined the *Glasgow Herald*. A *Scotsman* book critic found it 'exhilarating and urbane'. Their reactions demonstrate a continuing refusal to be miffed by insults which hurt – so long as they also amuse.

Some of Crosland's blunt arrows are harder to duck now than they were. He saw the Scotchman as a worthy peasant. 'As a hewer of wood and a drawer of water, as a person fitted by temperament for the exercise of mechanical functions, he is all very well; but in matters where intellect and wisdom are required he should be left severely alone. ' Crosland added: 'You will find that his only quality is his capacity for plod; as against this he has many ugly traits – jealousy, over-reachiness, and greediness among them.'

Jealous and greedy, OK. They are universal sins. In all honesty it is hard to concede that their tartan variety has a more lurid hue. Over-reachiness, however, is an accusation of a darker colour. It indicates bumptiousness and impidence. Maybe we do swagger. It's more certain that, when not full of a good conceit of ourselves, we sulk. And, maybe also, if we don't swagger, we'll perish. If we rattle our chains more heartily than subject tribes often do, it doesn't mean that we do not feel subjected. Over-reachiness and the self-advertisement that Crosland castigated can be only bad-mouth words for confidence. Strenuously now to cultivate the unspeakable qualities detected by Scotland's best critics would be an improvement. For taking pride in being called bumptious is to savour the taste of a missing ingredient.

On days when disappointment leaks into despair I take myself to a spot in the East End of Glasgow for the bleak comfort of confirming my feelings of dismay. At the feet of a statue in a bright shopping place I lay a tribute of gloomiest pessimism. Although the statue is a jolly sort of stookie, it is also a weed. It is out of place and totally out of order. Around it the new shops are called The Forge after Beardmore's Parkhead Forge, the wreck and rump of which occupied the site before the mall was built. Beardmore's was the biggest workshop of engineers and steelworkers anywhere. It was where was created the sinew that won the First World War. Giving the name of The Forge to the shopkeepers who have replaced the steelmen was a happy notion. They have created a lively, well-cherished place that is a pleasure to visit. As a discontinuation of a harsh and clarty past, sociable shopping is a welcome development. Less welcome is how a gigantic part of old Scotland has been not only erased, which can be hard enough to take, but insulted. History has been knocked wonky by that statue which confuses an industrial forge with a rural smiddy. To commemorate the armourers of empire has been put up a memorial to a village blacksmith in his shop making horseshoes. Heritage is further piddled upon by a wee dog at the smith's feet. One mercy is to be spared a chestnut tree. Beardmore's might as well never have been. It is a strange form of what the crusty Crosland saw as over-reachiness when a people stretch their imagination in order to pull out their roots. Impidence, yes. But whose? Benign ignorance resides closer to home than where it was found by the march of the miners of one generation ago. There are times at ye olde smiddy when it feels like a duty to weep.

ALLAN LAING

From Harry Lauder to Rab C. Nesbitt

Scottish Humour

A GOOD FEW YEARS AGO, SHORTLY BEFORE THE WORLD CUP IN SPAIN, THE Scottish football squad went to Canada, not to emigrate unfortunately, but to participate in some obscure warm-up tournament. For once the Tartan Army was nothing to write home about. There were only two of them.

The pair arrived in Toronto (or was it Vancouver?) and checked in to the cheapest rooming house they could find. Then, dressed in regulation denims and Scotland jerseys, they went off to the best hotel in the city – let us, for the sake of argument, call it the Toronto Hilton (or was it the Vancouver Hyatt?).

There – surprise, surprise – in the cocktail bar they found the SFA delegation, that dedicated band of followers without whom the wheels of Scottish football would grind to a halt. It was quickly pointed out to the Association panjandrums that, in their presence, was the entire travelling support. These two young men had sacrificed their hard-earned burroo money to follow Scotland to the Americas. The least they could do to show their appreciation was to buy the chaps a drink?

And they did just that. After one drink and ten minutes of patronising, hail-fellow-well-met conversation, the officials looked at their watches, said 'Good Lord, is that the time?' and swanned off to a big slap-up dinner somewhere else in the city. Unfortunately, one of the delegation had inadvertently left his room key on the table. The two fans battled with their conscience for all of a few seconds. Then they proceeded to wine and dine in style in the hotel, leaving the unsuspecting keyholder to foot the not insubstantial bill.

Later that night, their appetite sated and their thirst quenched, the boys thoughts turned to romance. Off they swanked to a nearby disco where, with that customary Scottish quick wit and repartee, they charmed the birds off the trees. Two young girls, to whom they had become attached, observed that their newly found companions were wearing Scotland strips. Not knowing that everyone and his brother wears Scotland strips in Scotland, they naturally assumed that the lads were *bona fide* members of the Scotland squad.

And so it was that the following day two unemployed teenagers from Castlemilk, both as thin as zips and between them not the size of tuppence, delivered a lecture to a captivated audience at a Canadian high school on the techniques and tactics of Scottish football. The headmaster later thanked Jim Leighton and Gordon Strachan for finding time in their busy schedule to address his pupils.

Now that, in the humble opinion of this writer, is a funny story. But it is really only funny because it is true. I know it happened because the two fans in question regaled me with the story one drunken night in a Torremolinos bar during the World Cup finals of 1982. It is funny because it is not a joke. No one wrote the script. And that is the beauty of Scottish humour. The truth never hurts . . . or at least it never hurts when you laugh. While other nations,

Billy Connolly, 1985.

particularly the bloody English, split their sides laughing at contrived gags, we find our humour in stories which are usually true though occasionally apocryphal.

During the last century, a pontificating old English humorist, by the name of Parson Sydney Smith was alleged to have remarked that it would require a surgical operation to get a joke into a Scotsman's head. Nothing, of course, could be further from the truth but his much-quoted insult must, even today, come as a great and abiding comfort to those (English) comedians who offer inanities as jokes only to discover that Scots don't laugh at them.

Actually, old Sid, God bless him, was misquoted. What happened was this. In conversation with Dr William Chambers, founder of *Chambers' Journal*, the parson was urged to admit that the Scots did indeed have a sense of humour.

'Yes,' replied Smith, 'you are an immensely funny people but you need a little operating on to let the fun out. I know no instrument so effectual for the purpose than a corkscrew.'

Maybe he had a point. A couple of drinks does tend to help us to see the funny side.

As a nation, however, we tend to loathe that awful English brand of humour, based around the clever pun and the slick small talk. We are too sophisticated for that nonsense. Old Sid was right. Perhaps we are difficult to amuse. But that does not mean that we are devoid of life's modulating and restraining balance wheel – a sense of humour.

The fact is that we are not given to over-enthusiasm. We are not into extrovert displays of wild chuckling laughter. We can't giggle on cue.

Someone once observed that 'the actor who, for an hour, pretends not to be able to keep his hat on, sends the Englishman into the seventh heaven of delight. Such a performance may make the Scotsman smile . . . but only out of pity.'

The 19th-century writer, Robert Ford, in his famous book on Scottish humour, *Thistledown*, summed it up like this: 'An Englishman's wit (he has little or no humour), being an acquired taste, comes out "on parade" while Scotch folks' humour, being the common gift of Nature to all and sundry in the land, slips out most frequently when and where least expected.'

I hate to return to Old Sid, who obviously didn't like us, but he declared that 'the only idea of wit which prevails occasionally in the North is laughing immoderately at stated intervals'. This, he said, was 'infinitely distressing to people of good taste.' That from a man who, if alive today, would find Bruce Forsyth, Bob Monkhouse and *Game for a Laugh* highly amusing.

His remark was a load of old tosh. The Scot is an epicure when it comes to humour and really only appreciates the finest of fun. That's why we appear morose to the English. No. Our laughs are like the visits of angels – few and far between. Maybe that's why the old Glasgow Empire was legendary as a graveyard for English comedians. They were brave men, standing up there on the stage, trying in vain to get a laugh from an audience which sat grim-faced and arms folded.

There is an old story which the great Sir Harry Lauder used to tell. He was once performing in Glasgow when he noticed in the front row of the stalls a wee woman. His eye was drawn to her because, no matter how many jokes he cracked, no matter how much the rest of the audience chuckled, the wee woman never smiled once. It was later, as the audience left the theatre, that the old dear turned to her pal and said: 'Aye, a grand wee comedian, yon man Lauder. But, oh my word, what an awfy job a had tae keep frae laughing.'

Lex McLean and friend Glen at the Pavilion, Glasgow, 1961.

*The immortal Chic
Murray, 1985.*

*Gregor Fisher, alias
Rab C. Nesbitt,
1987.*

Yes, we take our humour seriously. We are at once an earnest and a humorous nation, a pawky and self-analytical race. We are philosophers, one and all, and we are happiest when waxing lyrically about serious subjects like death and religion. Maybe it all goes back to our dreary Kirk background and our stern education system of the past. Our humour is rarely a joke. It is more often a comment on life.

The beauty of it all is its spontaneity; the utter want of effort to effect its production. We take unusual situations and relate them in a simple and matter-of-fact way. The aforementioned Scottish football supporters told their story sublimely. It came out as a matter of course and without the slightest indication on their part that they were aware of the beauty of their tale.

Scottish humour is gentle. It is of a quality, texture and dialect which the English find difficult to understand. We don't make jokes for effect and we are not so fond of the rapier-like wit of the English. The best of our humour falls naturally and often unconsciously without any effort. Sometimes it requires a second thought to fully realise its drift and the true value of its philosophical observations. Sometimes it seems our bounden duty to bring down anyone with airs and graces or ideas above their stations. Humour is a protean and elusive thing and we Scots should be thankful that we possess it in abundance.

So does anyone else like our humour? Well, yes. The Bulgarians, of course. Some years ago it was discovered that a town called Gabrovo in Bulgaria specialised in telling jokes about 'meanness'. It was the Aberdeen of the Eastern bloc. The link was apparently so strong that the press attache from the Bulgarian Embassy in London wrote to Scots contacts seeking Aberdeen joke books.

When you think about it, Scotland was probably the first European country to discover modern alternative comedy . . . maybe 50 years ago. Today there are dozens, if not hundreds, of fashionable young comics in the clubs of London who tell stories rather than deliver gags.

We've been doing it for a long time. It was Billy Connolly, I suppose, who started the modern version of the genre, though it has to be said that he owed a great debt to the legendary American humorist, Lenny Bruce. As a folk singer Connolly was average but the bits in between his songs made everybody laugh. They laughed because he did on stage what we all do in the pub. He told stories about his pals. And, when they dried up, he started commenting on the unusual, even unspeakable sides to life. He told them in that matter-of-fact way. They were not contrived. They never had punchlines. He was just another philosopher from Scotland.

Unfortunately for us, he chatted to Michael Parkinson on television and became 'The Big Yin', a sobriquet which sounds fine when it falls naturally from the tongue of a Glaswegian in a pub but sounds more like the title of a Chinese detective novel when delivered by an Englishman. Connolly never looked back, which is his loss.

Humour is a national characteristic. Every country, save perhaps Albania (I say that only because I imagine it), has its own. There is the predominantly Jewish humour of America, the satire of the French, the brutal bawdiness of the Australians. But there is nothing to compare to the humour of the Scots. That does not mean that we possess the finest sense of humour in the world. It just means that, well, there is nothing to compare it with.

When we laugh we laugh with and not at the object of our amusement. We are gentle and thoughtful, most of the time. We can get out of hand, of course. The drunken Scotsman is not always a figment of the foreigner's

'Auld Lang Syne' to the Empire Theatre, Glasgow, 1963.

Albert Finney says farewell to the famous Empire audience at the theatre's last show, Glasgow, 1963.

imagination. But even our drunks can be witty . . . maybe not clever, but witty.

I remember a wee Scots football supporter giving his account of the previous night's binge in some God-forsaken Continental holiday resort. 'There a wis, stumblin' intae a taxi an could a remember the name o' the hotel? Could a hell. An then it came tae me. A remembered the name frae the sign above the front lobby. So a says, "Take me tae the Hotel Receptioni, driver".'

The Scottish football supporter provides a wealth of examples of our sense of humour. A friend of mine from Glasgow, who worked in the British Consular Service in Madrid, was always given the task of looking after the football fans when they arrived for international matches in the city. On one particularly busy night, when Celtic were playing Real Madrid, he spent hours bailing out drunks from the local jails. He saw nothing of the game itself and, around midnight, he made his weary way home. He walked down the steps of the city's subway system to catch a late train. As he stood on the platform he noticed a solitary fan, lying sound asleep a few yards away. He thought about ignoring him but his conscience told him to do the decent thing.

My friend approached the lad, gave him a gentle kick to wake him up, and said: 'Hey, Jim. Where you going?'

The fan opened one eye, noticed he was in a subway station, and answered: 'Partick.'

I make no apology for returning to the Scots football fan, that dedicated follower of passion. To me he is the modern-day personification of our sense of humour. That is why, unlike his witless and often violent English counterpart, he is welcomed wherever in the world he may go. The Saltire counterpoint to the Union Jack hooligan.

Today there is a legion of young Scottish comedians performing, mostly in Glasgow. They may consider themselves to be alternative comics but, really, they are following in the finest tradition of Scottish humorists. As always, they reflect the politics and the feelings of the society in which they live. Therefore, they are socialists or nationalists . . . or both.

The best of our 20th-century comics have been working-class. We are essentially a working-class nation, after all. The cloth cap has been required dress for many . . . Chic Murray, Lex McLean, to name but two. Rikki Fulton and Jack Milroy charmed two generations as Francie and Josie, the East End jack-the-lads. Connolly came from the shipyards. Even our latest comedy manifestation, Rab C. Nesbitt, is the last word in Scottish working-class, i.e. unemployed.

Something occurs to me, looking at that last list of comedy greats. We Scots have a great tradition of finding a place in our hearts for our comedians, don't we? We are genuinely fond of them. We are loyal to them. Not only were we amused by the gentle tales of *Para Handy* on BBC Scotland, we were moved by them.

The funny business has changed in this day and age. Many of the old variety theatres and music halls have gone. Today our comics tour the pub circuit. Bruce Morton, one of the funniest of our new breed of stand-up comics, reckons that a comedian can really only consider himself successful when he has made, not the cover of *Rolling Stone*, but the centre pages of the *Daily Record*. To do that he needs television exposure. But Scottish television, so far, has taken few chances with modern humour. It has had its moments but, in general terms, it has not yet been prepared to deliver uncompromising programmes on essential modern comedy.

*Roddy McMillan
on the* Vital Spark,
1965.

And that, I suppose, is just about the story so far. It is a serious business, writing about comedy. It is, if you pardon the pun, no laughing matter.

No one is saying we Scots are perfect. We can be rude, abrasive, vulgar, thoughtless, and tasteless. But, for the most part, we are gentle and kind in our humour. When was the last time you heard a Scottish comedian, a good Scottish comedian, tell a racist or even a sexist joke?

It is reality upon which we dwell. Truth may well be stranger than fiction but truth is also infinitely funnier than manufactured circumstance.

And yet, when all is said and done, the key to successful comedy is based on universality. And a laugh is the same in any language.

Hugh MacDiarmid
(C. M. Grieve) with
a young Arnold
Wesker outside
Dungavel House,
1950.

*The West Highland
Line, 1988.*

Macbeth *at
Inchcolm, 1989.*

*The morning after
the party, New Year
at East Kilbride.*

*Former curator
Elspeth King dusts
down her People's
Palace, Glasgow,
1990.*

A silver lining to the street theatre, Edinburgh, 1989.

Designer Cindy Sirko at her tartan exhibition, Edinburgh, 1989.

Ravenscraig, 1989.

Out with the rubbish, George Square, Glasgow, New Year, 1990.

City of Culture,
Glasgow, 1990.

*Spey Valley floods,
Kingussie, 1989.*

*The Railway Bridge
at Inverness, 1989.*

Stornoway, Isle of Lewis, 1990.

Kirkwall Harbour, 1988.

*Patchwork in
Melville Street,
Edinburgh, 1989.*

*Marischal
College, Aberdeen
University, 1990.*

*Merchant City,
Glasgow, 1989.*

Dundee Harbour,
1990.

The Waverley *at Portree, Skye, 1989.*

Steaming through the Highlands, 1989.

*A colourful
conclusion to the
Rothesay revels,
1989.*

*The Paddle Steamer
Waverley at Skye,
1989.*

*Beer crates on
Calton Hill,
Edinburgh, 1989.*

*Fireworks on Princes
Street, Edinburgh,
1989.*

Garden allotments,
Dundee, 1990.

*John Paul Diamond
of Paisley is mascot
to the Johnstone
Pipe Band at
Bellahouston Park,
Glasgow, 1990.*

*The centenary
celebration of the
Forth Rail Bridge,
1990.*

*Going to the Mod,
Stornoway, Isle of
Lewis, 1989.*

*Penny for the Poll
Tax? Dalmarnock,
Glasgow, 1989.*

*George Mackay
Brown, Orkney,
1988.*

*Alasdair Gray at the
Necropolis, Glasgow,
1989.*

JACK McLEAN

We Came from Upper Scythia
The Scottish Mentality

'WE CAME FROM UPPER SCYTHIA AND TRAVELLED IN MANY LANDS,'
boasted the Scots in the Arbroath Declaration – the Scottish version of the
Magna Carta – and then, according to this historic document, we ended up in
Iberia, (the name – means 'Land of the Hebrew'). Later still the Scots settled in
Ireland. They called that 'Hibernia', also Land of the Hebrew. And then they
came to the land across the water, as a people written in the Latin transcription
of the original Erse, the Scots. So goes the legend, and a powerful legend, if in
the recent century somewhat scorned. Not scorned everywhere however. My
own father was convinced that he came from the scions of the Lost Tribe of
Israel and of Judah. Mind you, in typical Scots fashion he claimed that only
we McLeans of Duart were of the Chosen: as far as he was concerned the rest
of the natives of Scotland were unfortunate Gentiles. In common with most
Mullians – and indeed large numbers of West of Scotland Highlanders – my
father was small and dark and very Semitic-looking indeed. I have followed
him in physiognomy, though this has been assisted considerably by an actual
Jewish strain on the other side of my family tree. My father, however, was not
only convinced of the Lost Tribe status, he revelled in it altogether.

He was not alone in this. Norman Stone, the Glaswegian Professor of
Modern History at Oxford, once claimed that the Scots and the Jews were
the two greatest nations on Earth; that the two combined have given, man
for man, more to the sum of world experience than any other groupings of
peoples, and he may be right. Norman Stone has, like every Scot, an axe
to grind, but he is true enough as an historian in noting the remarkable
abilities of the Scots and the Jews to move everywhere and come up with
better lives for us all in the guise of economic advantage. Scots, like Jews,
are excellent financiers and honest bankers. In technology and the Sciences
it might just be argued that the Scots have the edge over their parent tribe.
In morality, stern and demanding, in Ethics and Philosophy, the Scots are
a mainspring in the very timepiece of such sciences, if sciences they be. The
Scottish Enlightenment we will come to at a later date. It may prove a case
for us.

Despite these intellectual advantages, or perhaps because of them, neither
the Scots nor the Jews are especially cultured in terms of the Arts. It is true
that Jews are prominent in the world of Music, but music is near to a science,
and a mathematick at that, and akin to thinking. The plastic arts and the
expression of the natural joy of and in life are largely unknown to Scots,
Jews, and to anybody who feels himself a part of the dispossessed. Some
Scots recognised this too. Lewis Grassic Gibbon did. Gibbon was himself,
in common with some of the Scottish intellectuals of his day (including
the charlatan Christopher Grieve), rather anti-Semitic and had a notion,
at least in early days, that the Nazis and Fascists could be supported. He
had this to say of Jews, or more particularly, Philistines: 'I have always
liked the Philistines, a commendable and gracious and cleanly race . . .'
He goes on to the Jews: 'And above, in the hills, in Jerusalem, dwelt the
Israelites, unwashed and unashamed, horrified at the clean anarchy which

WE CAME
FROM UPPER
SCYTHIA

66

A retired crofter,
Skye, 1975.

is the essence of life, oppressed by grisly fears of life and death and time, suborning simple human pleasures in living into insane debating on justice and right, the Good Life, the Soul of Man, artistic canon, aesthetic approach – and all the rest of the dirty little toys with which dirty little men in dirty little caves love to play . . .'

Lewis Grassic Gibbon (real name James Mitchell – interestingly his partner in crime, Grieve, saw fit to work under a pseudonym as well) was under the spell of the literary *vandervogel*, then fashionable, with its attendant fascistic authoritarianism. But how easy it was for a Scot to slide into such a posture. For who were Gibbon's Philistines, this cleanly race, if not the large-boned Teutons and Saxons and Picts? And were his Israelites but Scots, huddled in dark caves, picking away at their sensibilities and fear, like dirty fingernails scratching at scabs? Scabs of fears, of dark thoughts, of intelligences which the cleanly races did not and could not possess with their cleanly sing-songs round their campfires. It was the dark fears which produced the cities and the dirt no doubt; it was the dark fears which produced liberty and freedom and the even murkier ideas of What We Are. The Israelites and the Scots are concerned with the last more than anything else, and more than anyone else.

I have dwelt long on the Jews when I have talked of the Scots: this is right. For the Scots are a dispossessed people like the Jews, and essentially, if the history adumbrated by the Arbroath Declaration is to be believed, a nomadic race who have put down roots. Roots in a countryside barren and considered uninhabitable to easier, more 'cleanly', peoples. It is said there was a culture once in Scotland, clans were said to have arts of their own. This is not a piece of modern Scotland: it is not a piece of any history which the Scot of the last two centuries could recognise. The Scots are not the Irish. The Irish sing in a music-hall song: 'The strangers came and tried to tell us their ways/ They blamed us all for being what we are/ But you might as well go chasing after moonbeams/ Or light a penny-candle from a star.' There are no penny candles to light up the Caledonian penumbra of Calvinism, and there are never any moonbeams. The Scots are a depressed nation, but not an oppressed one. When the Irish – our cousins – threw off the psychological yoke of the English they revealed their lightness of heart. The Scots have no lightness of heart. Long, long ago they made their gloom official.

In part climate, in part history, the Scottish experience is one of hopelessness. For two centuries they had no politics. For two centuries the Scots had no office of State: they were ruled from outside. Men of ability either moved to London or further abroad and became – as they still contrive to do – part of the native ruling classes, or they stayed home and became nonentities. Or geniuses. This is what happened in the Scottish Enlightenment. This is what happened in the great schisms of the Scottish Church. There was simply no opportunity to make great upon the world's waters so the Scots talent drew itself to its own backyard and swam in puddles. And made waves at that, waves which were to eddy throughout the oceans.

Because the backyards were real enough. While the Scottish thinkers of the Enlightenment were exhibiting their genius there were other sources setting the Scots bang to rights and not in backyards but in kailyards. As it happens the 'Kailyard School' of literature, or indeed of thinking, was small, and consisted of a mere handful of practitioners. Yet, horribly, this influence was to spread throughout the entire nation, an influence far beyond whatever vitality it might once have possessed. To this day most of Scotland is in the thrall of kailyardism be it the *Sunday Post* and 'The Broons' or a

James Kelman,
writer, Glasgow,
1983.

*Ostaig steading at
Sleat, Skye, 1973.*

*New Year at George
Square, Glasgow,
1939.*

Hogmanay Horror Show on STV. Or what is worse, the urbanised version of Kailyardism, the Glasgow sentimentality which I dubbed with a phrase a long time back. I called it Black Sannyism.

'Jings, there we were skipping excitedly in oor wee black sannies, boatles of sugerally water in oor pockets, waiting for the train doon the Watter . . .' I ken it fine: I have written it often enough. The Black Sannies: a dead giveaway. Mollie Weir who earned her living these many years cleaning out English baths without scratching. An actress from Scotland, from, she said, the heartland of the Glasgow slums, showing us up with her voting English Tory and reminiscing about a Glasgow childhood in which the door was always open and the soup upon the hob and we were all that warm-hearted you would think that the Royal bloody Family were missing themselves not having a single-end in the middle of Dennistoun, just for the odd weekend like. You never heard such shite. I will tell you what the reality was. No I won't. Why should I? You can imagine it for yourselves.

But can the Scots imagine their own reality? I am unsure. Can they imagine their histories; their dreams? What dreams? What dream indeed. In the last 20 years we have seen a succession of interpreters of the Scots experience, and especially of the Glasgow experience. Many – most – of these novelists and playwrights who have laid claim to an interpretation of the Glasgow Kultur have come from outside of that city. William McIlvanney has written rather ludicrously of the underlying violence of Glasgow and has relished every word of his fantasy. He has glorified hardmen when those of us brought up in the dank slums knew them for the pathetic mountebanks they were and were afeard of them. He came with his Kilmarnock bunnet and looked at the bright lights of the only city he had ever been in and stood in his Yooni blazer and said: 'This is the Big Toun.' I will not be too harsh on Mr McIlvanney, for he followed many another like him.

Lady poets wrote of Glasgow and the toughness from their West-End fastnesses, and romanticised in smart bars with like-minded voyeurs. Alasdair Gray became internationally known partly because of his undeniable talent, but much because Glasgow and its so-called vitality was a marketable idea. James Kelman, another novelist on the Glasgow scene, has been put up for the Booker Prize, for heaven's sake, because he is said to write in the Glasgow demotic and it is interesting to the jaded littérateurs of the metropolitan scene. Black Sannyism all of it. It might just as well be *No Mean City*, written with more expertise and even less honesty. It might just as well be Mollie Weir, scratching endlessly at her employer's bath.

And worse. Glasgow, the upas tree itself, has not merely consumed the west and the central industrial belt; it has consumed the rest of the country too. You will have to look to a body over 40 in Portree to hear a Skye accent. The younger folk speak Glasgow-style, just as the bucolic peasantry in Norfolk will intone in deepest Cockney: they get it off the telly. Sure you will find regionalism where the Poujade-ism is a little stronger. Open up a Scottish wireless of a Sunday morning and you will find spread before you a conscious effort at being yer ain folk: it would drive you daft. The peasant music now expressing itself through the jiggly piano-accompaniment and the fiddle vibrato shaking with last night's bevvy and the ever-present accordion is said to be traditional. It is as traditional as wee lassies with pudding faces slapping bales of tartan waste between each other and giving out heederum-hoederums and the Gaelic Mod with the pudding-faced wee girls now grown up and with complacencies to match the size of their tits. Gaelic speakers determined to prove that their culture is a match for the Quattrocento. As traditional as the idea of equality in Scottish schools and

Archie Hind, author of The Dear Green Place, *Glasgow, 1984.*

the Royal Highs and Fettes and Glenalmonds to prove it. A bloody lie, the lot.

Especially Scottish egalitarianism; especially that. My intemperance in the above paragraph will tell you quite a lot about egalitarianism. When I was a boy there was a considerable regard for democracy where I lived. I went to an egalitarian, if meritocratic, school. I felt no other my superior wherever he lived. My working-class and deprived background was no different from anybody else's and I was too late to romanticise it as the younger people did. It took me years to discover that that was a myth too. A deprived background became almost compulsory. If you were going to be a writer, an interpreter of the Scottish scene, you would have to be working class, with outside lavvies and all your teeth out by the age of 21. Glasgow, working class, crude, vomit on a Hogmanay pavement: this was what passed for our culture, if it wasn't wee fat girls with well-brushed hair chanting meaningless sibilants in a municipal hall in Dundee which smells, as indeed Scottish culture itself does, of Domestos and complacency. When are the Scottish middle classes going to assert themselves in our culture as they do in the rest of the British Isles – James Joyce was by no means a proletarian – when are the bourgeoisie going to do anything more than make money and get upset when their errant daughters marry unsuitable folk like darkies or bus conductors or maybe the both together?

Scottish culture consists, when it is not abroad and exercised by expatriates, of Hogmanay sentimentalism, heavy drinking, punitive sentencing, and a sometimes justified conceit of its legal system. Scots are by nature law-abiding which is why transgression, committed by a few, is so heavily punished. What it does not possess at all is a series of expressions such as music, painting, literature, film, or very much imagination. Or at least rarely, and very rarely indeed when it comes to global recognition. The Scots are an important people when it comes to their contributions world-wide yet no one recognises the Scot.

The Irish, yes. The Polish and Italian emigrant eminence is understandable for they are large nations with different languages from the English spoken in the Second World. But why the Irish? In the last two hundred years more people have emigrated from Scotland per head of population than any other country in Europe and none has had such effect in the industry and economy. Yet the Scots world image consists of a vague feeling that the menfolk wear kilts and the Highlands have mist-shrouded castles. Ask a European about Scotland and he is as mystified as, well, mist would make you.

Scotland is a small country after all, but it is not as small as, say, Ireland, and that country has done infinitely more to establish itself not only as a culture, but its inhabitants, wherever they are, as a nation. I keep on coming back to Ireland. Scotland is not two-thirds of a population of that island across from it and huge numbers of the Scottish nation are from Irish stock within memory and yet Ireland has an identifiable culture and Scotland has not. Ireland itself has little culture save literature and its sons and daughters have more often than not been forced to flee to be recognised.

Yet Scotland has no artistic culture which is recognised at all, at least until recently. Recently now. Recently there have been painters and artists, most of them part of a fashion boom. Recently there have been writers and playwrights and the same can probably be said for them too. Some of our most profound artists and thinkers have been disregarded for so long they have given up. Novelist Archie Hind who wrote the most seminal book since the war, *The Dear Green Place*, says he has given up. The very title of his novel is now used so commonly that few people even realise that he damn-near invented it. Hind's subsequent career does not suggest there is much of a future for the Scottish intellectual. He is now a perspicacious book reviewer for a prominent Scottish paper. He was once a perspicacious writer of the sort of books he now reviews. But then, Scotland is a profoundly Philistine country, not in the cleanly way which Lewis Grassic Gibbon ludicrously considered, but in the flat and money-tempered methodology of an Ebenezer Balfour determined to lead his nephew to his doom on a rotten staircase with nothing but a flickering candle to light his way.

This is the Scottish dichotomy and its antizyssygy; in the midst of Glaswegian gaiety, desperate and frantic, is gloom and they are both the same coin. For like the Israelites, the Scots have darkness in their minds. Culture, the Arts, is seen as bright rouge on the skull of human despair. In the middle of country pragmatism and Highland cunning is Celtic despondency and worse. The Scots are indeed like the Jews. They have too great a sense of themselves, and sadly not enough. There is very little fun. It is no joke to be a Scot.

'The sky is blue, the grass is green . . .'. Hallowe'en, Glasgow, 1954.

LESLEY DUNCAN

Jock Tamson's Bairns

A Scottish Childhood

MONSTERMAN, AGED 11, PREPARES FOR SCHOOL. HE PREENS HIMSELF
in the mirror. Hair gel is liberally applied to the salon-cut locks. Has
he discovered girls (as distinct from being co-educated with them since
kindergarten)? Probably not. He is just responding to peer group pressure.
That also accounts for the caterwaulings of the cult pop group on the purloined
family stereo whose leads snake from the lad's bedroom. 'It's cool, Mum.'

The young sophisticate's image is slightly spoiled by the mess of congealed
sweetie papers, erasers and pencil stubs I have just removed from his blazer
pockets. The schoolbag – not leather but gaudy nylon – spills its trail of
dog-eared exercise books, paper aeroplanes, dictionaries and *Dandys*. There's
still a reassuring touch of Oor Wullie (or do I just mean William?) about this
offspring of mine, this Scottish child, vintage 1990.

But is there much that is uniquely Scottish about childhood in Scotland
today? Far less, I would guess, than for my own 11-year-old self in
what Monsterman (alias David) terms 'the olden days'. Days of Attlee
and austerity, though days maybe sweetened for adults by the lingering
camaraderie of wartime.

We children, unassailed by television's glib global images, were little aware
of matters political, social or economic. We went about the business of being
young with total self-absorption, the centres of our small universes of school,
home, and playtime.

While the *haute bourgeoisie* of Scotland's cities, even 40 years ago, sent
their children to one-sex, fee-paying schools, the norm for children of
smaller towns and rural communities was comprehensive co-education.
Perhaps this Knoxian tradition, much debased now by sociological cant,
did offer something unique to the Scottish child.

At the red-sandstone primary school in the seaside burgh of Troon, the
emphasis was on the currently unfashionable numeracy and literacy. Our
minds were honed on mental arithmetic, grammar, parsing, and sentence
analysis – grounding which still proves valuable for telling who is really
whom and for strangling dangling participles at birth. That modern shibboleth
'creative expression' had not yet been invented to perplex the kindly, if stern,
schoolmarms who ruled our days, but we read omnivorously, everything
from Dundee comics to Dumas novels of intrigue and skulduggery at the
Valois court (much more bloodthirsty than anything the Tudors got up
to).

My classmates had resonant names like Wallace Edminston, Beatrice
Ballingall and Kathleen Plenderleith. Where are they now, I wonder?
Probably scattered round the globe in the Scots diaspora. My own class
sported an unusual number of left-handed youngsters. Children destined
for the professions or to work in the local co-op shops at 15 shared their
formative years and frequent ministrations of the belt, a punishment given
and accepted without malice as part of the scheme of things.

Since this was an Ayrshire school, there were annual Burns competitions –
which ensured that at least one Burns poem and song went into the collective

*American Air Force
family at Prestwick,
1957.*

consciousness each year. So we tossed our heads to 'Comin' Through the Rye', ha-ha'ed over Duncan Gray's wooing, soared effortfully to the top notes of 'My Luve Is Like a Red Red Rose'. And there were prizes; no inhibitions in those days about singling out merit. The Burns cult was certainly a uniquely Scottish aspect of childhood.

So too, in retrospect, was the double language of many of the children, the vernacular of the playground and the short-vowelled standard English of the classroom. Writers like William McIlvanney have written with passion about the attempt to suppress Scottish children's natural self-expression. Teachers and parents still face the dilemma of whether to constrict the young, for their own sake, to the English-speaking norm. Can one draw a distinction between acceptable Scottish idiom – the 'kens' and 'taes' of traditional speech and the merely slovenly like 'I seen' and 'I done'? It would be good to think so.

In any case I doubt if my classmates who could shift effortlessly from demanding one 'gi'e them a len' o' somethin' ', to reciting how Horatio held the bridge, suffered from linguistic schizophrenia. After all, small nations who cohabit with big ones have always had to make cultural accommodations. The Czechs had to espouse Russian in addition to German when they exchanged Austro-Hungarian for Soviet dominance. Yet many Czechs manage to be eloquent in English too. Perhaps, indeed, the ability to swap languages easily will be a positive benefit to young Scots in the EC days ahead. Even the dreaded glottal stop could be an asset in wrapping the tongue round Russian!

Whether they passed 'the qualifying' or not, the children of Troon graduated automatically to Marr College. The copper-domed school was the altruistic legacy of a coal merchant who wanted to see millionaires' daughters educated with dustmen's sons. In superb wood-panelled classrooms, and under the tutelage of a distinguished teaching staff, the democratic intellect did indeed flourish. Generations of boys and girls whose fathers worked in the local shipyard or railway works, competed, and more than held their own, with the children of the wealthy and privileged. Girls were expected to shine at mathematics and science. They did.

Svengali'd through Higher Maths by 'Chucky' Peebles, initiated into the niceties of Verlaine and Victor Hugo by Dr Philippe le Harivel, numerous children from 'working-class' backgrounds graduated from university and into the professions. It was a story paralleled, of course, in academies and high schools throughout Scotland, though the amenities of Marr and the little town's social mix made ideal conditions for success.

One group of children were, sadly, missing from this rosy picture – the Catholic children, self-exiled to a school in the neighbouring town. It seems a shame that they missed the facilities of Marr and that we missed their company.

Scottish education has in recent times been under siege from educational influences from the South. But in my schooldays at least there were links with a wider European cultural inheritance. Each summer, school children from Ayrshire shared summer camps (the bivouacking connotations are hardly fair to the former nunnery in Versailles) with teenagers from various parts of France. There must have been an intellectual disparity between the schoolboys and girls of small-town Ayrshire and the budding *baccalauréat*-sitters of Paris and Lyons and Clermont-Ferrand. The memory of the camp song is hopelessly entangled with the *Marseillaise* in my mind but the final flourish, 'L'Ecosse est belle et vive la France!' seems fair.

No doubt the Scottish youngsters had their horizons widened by the close encounters with French manners and mores, not to say plumbing.

Jiving at the
American Air Force
base, Monkton,
1956.

And at least one of Scotland's distinguished Continental exports, the poet Kenneth White, of the Sorbonne, shared this experience. For me it led to pen-friendships with two erudite French girls (one born in the Pripet Marshes) and a blissful student summer spent in the Pyrenees.

They didn't teach us the words of 'Auld Lang Syne' at school (an accurate knowledge of the chorus would have been handy for future revellers) but the central verses capture something central to Scottish childhood – the direct, artless contact with nature. 'We twa hae run about the braes,/ And pou'd the gowans fine', and 'We twa hae paidl'd in the burn,/ Frae morning sun till dine', Burns wrote in his salute to friendship. Most non-city Scottish children have had the chance to wade in burns, scramble in open countryside. Even the areas of north Lanarkshire most desecrated by 19th-century industrialisation abutted on wilderness.

The burn and moor of my own childhood were miniature ones, engulfed now in suburban housing, but then offering endless scope for games of the imagination. We played cowboys and Indians among the whin bushes with their astonishing spring saffroning, built camp fires, dammed the burn, tunnelled through bramble patches with resultant rips to clothing and limbs. We hunted for edible soorocks among the pink-seeded meadow grass, sometimes taking with us flower or bird books in a half-hearted gesture to self-improvement. Still, the spotting of a yellowhammer or a grounded cuckoo added to the pattern of these days as much as the sight of harebells quivering in the August wind.

That wind was almost always a south-westerly, sweeping up the Clyde estuary, bending the hawthorn hedges and sycamore shelter belts before it. The seashore was also our domain. Its ribbed sands and shallow pools were considered a safe playground, even if the outfall from sewage pipes reinforced the natural fringe of seaweed. There was also in my youngest days the detritus of war – oranges from sunk cargo boats, the occasional mine. We survived such hazards, practising swimming underwater with eyes open or floating precariously on our backs. When we finally emerged, shivering and ravenous, it was to gobble the 'chittery bites' provided by our mothers.

Perhaps these sorties explain my adult response to the pictures of the great William McTaggart, who could, when not storm-tossed, imply most magically the meeting point of sand and water. He often painted in Kintyre, on the other side of the firth. Arran lay between, an island real and visitable but also a potent place of dreams. Its central peaks, Cir Mhor and Goatfell, and the humped spine of the Sleeping Warrior could have sprung from a Tolkien map. North of the Cock of Arran, insubstantial as a mirage, were the Paps of Jura and beyond them America.

The jets of the American Air Force base at Prestwick added to the western perspective of childhood, as did the New York and Toronto-bound passenger planes. Some of my former schoolmates married Americans from the air base, sustaining the traditional links of the West of Scotland with the New World. Others, myself included, went to the United States or Canada for post-graduate studies or to dodge National Service.

That was for the future. Meanwhile we enjoyed, in that lovely phrase of Seamus Heaney's, a feral childhood. There were other entertainments. Through the cinema, images of America – the canyons of New York, the dusty reaches of the Wild West (usually a back lot in Hollywood, but we were not to know that) were locked permanently into our heads. 'Mr Bluebird on my shoulder,/ It's the truth essential,/ Everything is satisfactory . . .' sang the cognoscenti of the playground within weeks of *Oklahoma!*'s première. We played peevers, stotted balls off the school

Cranston's Tea
Rooms at the corner
of Queen Street and
Argyle Street.

Thrills of the 'Rotor'
at the carnival,
Glasgow Green,
1953.

walls, indulged in unintentional aerobics with skipping ropes. In winter days of frost and chilblains the playground was treacherous with slides.

The 'shows' came annually – latterly dispatched to a site between the gasworks and the municipal coup by a disapproving council. The tawdry roundabouts and shooting galleries, the whiff of wildness and danger from the fairground people themselves, fascinated the young.

Hallowe'en, even in my childhood, was a shadow of its former self. We did, it's true, dress up and, chaperoned by an adult, visit neighbours' houses, reciting rhymes about wee freendly dugs or bogles by boortrees, and receiving (as the reward for stopping?) money, tablet or apples. Now the ghoulish night has been displaced in my corner of central Scotland by Guy Fawkes capers. What's left of the genuine Hallowe'en tradition has been corrupted by an imported American perception of the same, complete with tricks or treats. There are even pumpkins on sale at the supermarkets. Unfair exchange for the leering turnip-heids of yore.

The main family celebration of our year was Christmas, though Great Uncle Alec – a mining engineer who had gained a comfortable income and lost an alarming number of finger-tips pursuing his career in Spain – sent and expected New Year cards.

Cousins, aunts and uncles foregathered at my maternal grandmother's home. Tall and stately, with brown almond-shaped eyes, she was not the kind of granny one would ever have contemplated pushing off a bus. She was a Bone from Ayrshire, a name I inherited and winced at through childhood. The artistic handle seems pleasing now.

It is mainly granny's cooking that I remember: superb shortbread; impenetrable black bun; salty broth. Grandfather was by physical contrast a skelf of a man with a weak heart that saw him through 80 years, cold blue eyes, and a limited tolerance for the young. Still, he did introduce us to alcohol in a civilised way with thimblefuls of sherry in his best crystal glasses on the 25th. The pair were avid readers, he on one side of the fireplace with Dickens, she on the other with Scott.

Dumpling was the highlight of the Christmas feast. How I hated the insertion of threepenny bits, however hygienically wrapped. How I panicked, lest a cousin receive a larger slice of the succulent spice-and-raisin-stuffed dessert, which looked rather like a soggy curling stone. I have long since succumbed for convenience to the pallid English substitute of Christmas pudding. The Dutch, I've been told, also make dumpling on special days. Is this yet another Scottish tradition with Continental links?

My father's parents were dead before I was born but grandfather Munn left legends behind. He was a stationmaster. In his 70s he acquired a racing cycle on which he peddled furiously round the back roads of Renfrewshire. He also was an enthusiastic reader and one day almost allowed my then-infant brother to drown in a bowl of custard while his own head was stuck in a book. Was it Cremola custard? I expect so.

My father followed him into railway employment, though he dearly wanted to go to art school, and spent his free time roaming the hills of Ayrshire, fishing rod and sketch pad to hand. We lived close to the Glasgow–Stranraer railway line – which perhaps explains why steam engines still haunt my subconscious. The real things were heroic enough – ominous cylinders tilting round the curve, belching smoke and steam, to stop at Barassie station, or distantly traversing the green, rolling Ayrshire countryside, streamers of white dissolving behind them.

The old LMS carriages (inexplicably first and third class) were divided into compartments sporting sepia photographs of Llandudno and the Lake

Glasgow Green 'shows', 1960.

Glasgow Green 'shows', 1974.

JOCK
TAMSON'S
BAIRNS

84

*Preparing for
Bonfire Night,
Glasgow, 1951.*

*Hallowe'en,
Hamilton, 1940.*

St Paul's Episcopal Church Hallowe'en Party, Aberdeen, 1946.

District. The compartments were good for card schools, also for part-singing. My brother and I used to air our version of the theme and descant from Bizet's 'L'Arlesienne Suite' *en route* for Paisley or Glasgow.

One day a gaunt, black-bearded giant entered our compartment. I'm not sure how we recognised Douglas Young, modern Makar and author of 'The Minister said it waid deel' that black little poem on the thrawnness of fate. I was overcome with nervous giggles, much to my family's and the bard's discomfiture. Similar untimely laughter overtook me in Red Square two decades later at the sight of the pickled Lenin.

Rail expeditions to Glasgow offered the bait of refreshments at Craig's tearooms. The Rhul, at the eastern end of Sauchiehall Street, was a particular favourite. How civilised the vanished tearooms of Glasgow were, and not just those decorated by Mackintosh for Miss Cranston. The Rhul had shiny dark woodwork, white linen and towering silver cake stands. It mattered little if the Bath buns were stodgy. They could be consumed in the company of paintings of the Glasgow School – soulful David Gauld cattle, Stuart Park rose studies, Walton landscapes, too, I recall. My mother had taken classes with Park at Glasgow School of Art, which did not stop her viewing his work with a critical eye.

Today there are Pizzalands and Burger Kings and McDonalds to feed hungry young Scots. In their eating habits they are true internationalists now. Even Moscow has its Big Mac.

In so many ways today's children are more globally knowledgeable than those of 'the olden days'. Television is, of course, the main culprit or benefactor. Even with reasonably controlled viewing children are bound to see news bulletins and have their emotions jolted – however briefly – by images of earthquake, famine, political upheaval.

Much of the knowledge and the emotional impact is superficial, as it is with adult viewers. There is even the argument that exposure to distressful pictures can harden emotional arteries, that finally we view the most harrowing images as aspects of entertainment. Against that, perhaps even superficial knowledge or concern is better than none. To have cried once over a skeletal Ethiopian contemporary or fleetingly pitied a Romanian baby, as many Scottish children like mine must have done in recent times, is surely better than not to have done so at all?

And perhaps these children of ours, blasé as they are about electronic gadgetry, mesmerised as they seem to be by the siren voices of pop, have more tender hearts and the potential for being better world citizens than their adults. The price may be the loss of innocence and the diminishing of their own cultural background. How sad.

Happy New Year, Glasgow, 1957.

JOHN LINKLATER

The Literary Landscape

Scotland: Fact or Fiction?

WHEN ALAN SHARP SET *A GREEN TREE IN GEDDE* (1965) IN A TOWN CALLED
Greenock he was breaking an established convention. Since the 1820s, when
John Galt was inventing new names for every town and village in Ayrshire,
Scottish writers had been advised to dive for fictional cover when dealing
with places. Only Glasgow and Edinburgh were regarded as big enough (or
anonymous enough?) to resist being called anything else, except by writers
of genius. Alasdair Gray made the former the City Of Unthank in *Lanark*
(1981). Robert Louis Stevenson pulled off a remarkable coup in *The Strange
Case of Dr Jekyll and Mr Hyde* (1886) disguising his stated fixation with
low-life Edinburgh's 'lighted streets and the swinging gait of harlots' by
pretending to write about London. This more than satisfied the Scottish
demand for places to be rendered under an alias.

It never seemed to matter if these fictional places could be identified by
shrewd readers. When an obvious hometown found its way into fiction it
was still better for the writer to adopt a veneer of coyness, no matter how
ludicrous. If a man belonged to a coastal village like Dunbeath, Caithness,
and wrote about a fishing village which he called 'Dunster' (as Neil Gunn did
in *Silver Darlings* in 1941) there was, admittedly, a fair chance that someone
might catch on. But the point was a legal one. Giving places their real names
was only offering opportunity to the litigious real people who might find
themselves in the novel.

The smaller the community the greater the degree the writer is cautioned
to adopt the line stated in the title of Douglas Dunn's short story collection,
Secret Villages (1985). In Scotland there might well be a shortage of decent
names to go round as a character observes in one of Dunn's stories, but
playing about with Gaelic prefixes and suffixes usually provides something.
Nevertheless the writer is advised to be careful about following the George
Friel method too closely. He came up with 'Tordoch' to name a housing
scheme in Glasgow in *Mr Alfred M.A.* (1972) – not so much a disguise as a
translation: tor/hill, dubh/dark.

There was playful subtlety in such a lapse, and we struggle to find the
same in Sharp's giving the name Greenock to the Greenock in his book. A
solution was discovered 14 years later by Robin Jenkins when he borrowed
the name Gantock from a local hotel and applied it to the Greenock of
his excellent novel, *Fergus Lamont* (1979). But the only previous model
available to Sharp was Edwin Muir, and this was a highly confusing one.
In *An Autobiography* (1954) Muir demonstrated a very sure touch, getting
all sorts of places like Glasgow, London, Prague, Dresden and Rome right,
and giving them chapters to themselves. But when he came to Greenock, to
which he devoted chapter four, he stumbled. There was no need for him to
suddenly resort to fictionalisation. Even Scots readers are tolerant of the
naming of real places in non-fiction. When he called the place Fairport it
was probably less a case of dreadful amnesia as indulgence in heavy irony.
His experience of Greenock, working in a bone factory in his early 1920s,
had been anything but fair. By calling it Fairport he was probably also saying

*Neil Gunn examines
the film of* Silver
Darlings, *Caithness,
1951.*

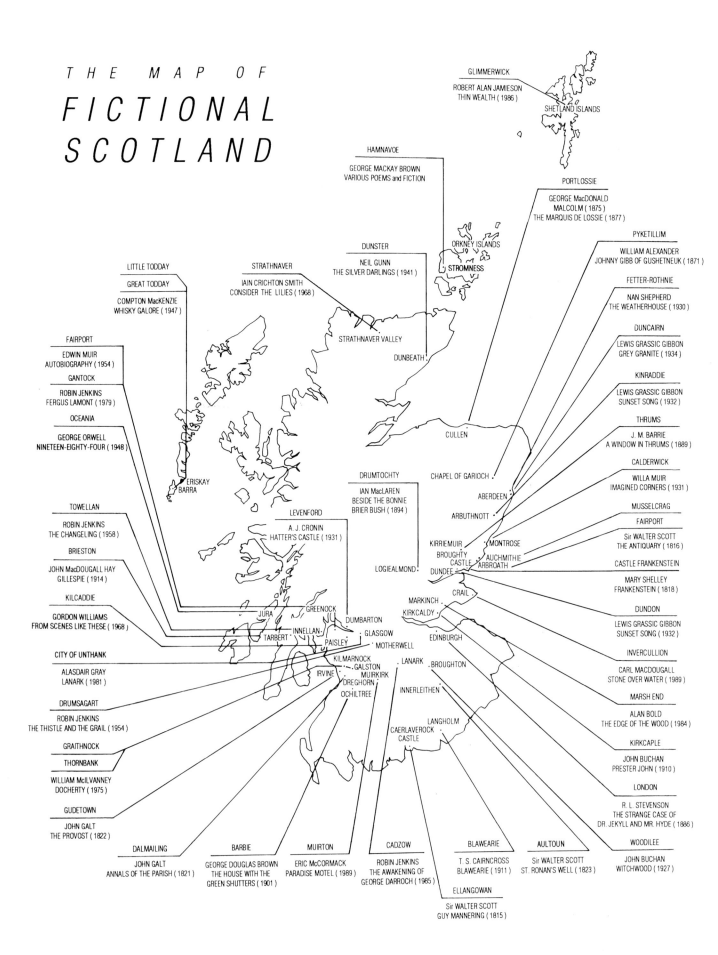

THE MAP OF
FICTIONAL
SCOTLAND

GLIMMERWICK
ROBERT ALAN JAMIESON
THIN WEALTH (1986)

SHETLAND ISLANDS

HAMNAVOE
GEORGE MACKAY BROWN
VARIOUS POEMS and FICTION

PORTLOSSIE
GEORGE MacDONALD
MALCOLM (1875)
THE MARQUIS DE LOSSIE (1877)

ORKNEY ISLANDS
STROMNESS

DUNSTER
NEIL GUNN
THE SILVER DARLINGS (1941)

PYKETILLIM
WILLIAM ALEXANDER
JOHNNY GIBB OF GUSHETNEUK (1871)

LITTLE TODDAY
GREAT TODDAY
COMPTON MacKENZIE
WHISKY GALORE (1947)

STRATHNAVER
IAIN CRICHTON SMITH
CONSIDER THE LILIES (1968)

FETTER-ROTHNIE
NAN SHEPHERD
THE WEATHERHOUSE (1930)

DUNCAIRN
LEWIS GRASSIC GIBBON
GREY GRANITE (1934)

FAIRPORT
EDWIN MUIR
AUTOBIOGRAPHY (1954)

STRATHNAVER VALLEY

DUNBEATH

KINRADDIE
LEWIS GRASSIC GIBBON
SUNSET SONG (1932)

GANTOCK
ROBIN JENKINS
FERGUS LAMONT (1979)

THRUMS
J. M. BARRIE
A WINDOW IN THRUMS (1889)

OCEANIA
GEORGE ORWELL
NINETEEN-EIGHTY-FOUR (1948)

CALDERWICK
WILLA MUIR
IMAGINED CORNERS (1931)

ERISKAY
BARRA

CULLEN

DRUMTOCHTY
IAN MacLAREN
BESIDE THE BONNIE
BRIER BUSH (1894)

CHAPEL OF GARIOCH

MUSSELCRAG
FAIRPORT
Sir WALTER SCOTT
THE ANTIQUARY (1816)

TOWELLAN
ROBIN JENKINS
THE CHANGELING (1958)

ABERDEEN

ARBUTHNOTT

LEVENFORD
A. J. CRONIN
HATTER'S CASTLE (1931)

CASTLE FRANKENSTEIN
MARY SHELLEY
FRANKENSTEIN (1818)

BRIESTON
JOHN MacDOUGALL HAY
GILLESPIE (1914)

KIRRIEMUIR
BROUGHTY
CASTLE
LOGIEALMOND
DUNDEE

MONTROSE
AUCHMITHIE
ARBROATH

KILCADDIE
GORDON WILLIAMS
FROM SCENES LIKE THESE (1968)

DUNDON
LEWIS GRASSIC GIBBON
SUNSET SONG (1932)

CRAIL
MARKINCH
KIRKCALDY

JURA
GREENOCK
DUMBARTON

CITY OF UNTHANK
ALASDAIR GRAY
LANARK (1981)

INVERCULLION
CARL MACDOUGALL
STONE OVER WATER (1989)

EDINBURGH

INNELLAN
TARBERT
GLASGOW
PAISLEY
MOTHERWELL

LANARK
BROUGHTON

MARSH END
ALAN BOLD
THE EDGE OF THE WOOD (1984)

DRUMSAGART
ROBIN JENKINS
THE THISTLE AND THE GRAIL (1954)

KILMARNOCK
GALSTON
MUIRKIRK
IRVINE
DREGHORN
OCHILTREE

INNERLEITHEN

KIRKCAPLE
JOHN BUCHAN
PRESTER JOHN (1910)

GRAITHNOCK
THORNBANK
WILLIAM McILVANNEY
DOCHERTY (1975)

LANGHOLM
CAERLAVEROCK
CASTLE

LONDON
R. L. STEVENSON
THE STRANGE CASE OF
DR. JEKYLL AND MR. HYDE (1886)

GUDETOWN
JOHN GALT
THE PROVOST (1822)

WOODILEE
JOHN BUCHAN
WITCHWOOD (1927)

DALMAILING
JOHN GALT
ANNALS OF THE PARISH (1821)

BARBIE
GEORGE DOUGLAS BROWN
THE HOUSE WITH THE
GREEN SHUTTERS (1901)

MUIRTON
ERIC McCORMACK
PARADISE MOTEL (1989)

CADZOW
ROBIN JENKINS
THE AWAKENING OF
GEORGE DARROCH (1985)

BLAWEARIE
T. S. CAIRNCROSS
BLAWEARIE (1911)

AULTOUN
Sir WALTER SCOTT
ST. RONAN'S WELL (1823)

ELLANGOWAN
Sir WALTER SCOTT
GUY MANNERING (1815)

he could not believe Greenock at all.

It was a feeling shared by Sharp, who received his education there. Despite his novel's double-edged and prophetic dedication: 'to Greenock, to its buildings and chimneys and streets and the glimpses they have afforded me of the river and the hills', he had never come to terms with the town as a real place. The Greenock skyline merely led the eye out over the River Clyde and beyond. If it served any purpose at all it was as a vehicle for transcendental meditation, and Sharp had greater faith in the places the mind reached. This is a theme of the novel. Such a transcendental landfall is achieved by the character Gibbon. 'You will not find it down on any map,' he says. 'True places never are.'

Sharp thanked Greenock for letting him see the river and the trees and caught the plane for Hollywood, a place where fantasy is the main industry. At least one of its products might have been commissioned by the Scottish Tourist Board: the sometime Highlands village of Brigadoon.

We must not blame the Americans. Some of Scotland's most alert imaginations have addressed themselves to the task of dredging film rights out of the swamp of our caricatured culture. Compton Mackenzie was even prepared to drag himself away from an active role in the Scottish Nationalist movement to pour himself a Great Todday and a Little Todday out of the islands of Barra and Eriskay in *Whisky Galore* (1947), a novel so facile it earned him a knighthood. A. J. Cronin found that the easiest place to find filmable books was in other people's novels, borrowing one of John Gourlay's commercial carts to haul the 'Barbie' of *The House With The Green Shutters* (1901) up to Dumbarton. But the fictional town in *Hatter's Castle* (1931) was of his own coinage: 'Levenford'. Then he gave the world 'Tannochbrae' to cap a brilliant literary career. Bill Forsyth has carried on this grand tradition by giving us 'Ferness', reputedly on the Buchan coasts in the enchanting film 'Local Hero' (1983).

Bad writing is a serious business. Edwin Morgan is not alone in asking if it does not fulfil some special need in the Scottish soul. What other explanation can be found for the kailyard schools except profound cynicism? Morgan was examining the fictions which emerge from Ian Maclaren's 'Drumtochty', modelled on Logiealmond, Perthshire, and J. M. Barrie's 'Thrums', modelled on Kirriemuir anecdotes handed down by the author's mother. A typical theme, devised by Morgan, 'might show the "lad o' pairts" in some country village who is carefully nurtured by the local dominie and minister, goes to university in a city like Glasgow, and quickly dies of consumption, perhaps with a ray of light from the setting sun falling neatly on his calm white face as he expires'.

This description carries far too much accuracy for comfort. Note Morgan's telling use of 'like Glasgow'. His objection to kailyard fiction is its failure to acknowledge or portray underlying social conditions. Death from tuberculosis was prevalent in Glasgow tenements. Readers of kailyard fiction might be led to believe people died for sentimental reasons.

Morgan's indignation is useful and exemplary. There is a danger of allowing it to become critically fashionable to make kailyardism worthy of serious attention. An American professor, who just happens to have written the only critical study devoted at book length to the history of Scottish fiction (Francis Russell Hart, *The Scottish Novel: From Smollett To Spark*, 1978) expressed disappointment that Scottish readers had failed to recognise the true symbolic purpose of kailyard fiction as the search for a lost Eden. Douglas Gifford dismissed this thesis out of hand in his 1981 lecture 'The Dear Green Place?'. He demonstrated that it was

Edwin Muir at home in Newbattle Abbey College, 1951.

impossible to move across the fictional map of Scotland without colliding with writers searching for a lost Eden. The theme is older than kailyardism, older than the hills in which many of these searches are conducted. And it is a theme which resurfaces time and again in serious contemporary fiction, notably in Robin Jenkins. William McIlvanney searches for lost values in his fictional working-class communities of 'Graithnock', based on Kilmarnock, and 'Thornbank', which could be Galston, and he forces his characters to discover new personal moralities through conflict with the old. George Mackay Brown searches for timeless Edens, and employs the deliberate archaic form of 'Hamnavoe', for Stromness, to emphasise the superimpositions of past, present and future, myth and reality. The search for Eden, or trying to lose hell: it's the same thing, and it covers most Scottish fiction.

What else do you expect in the literature of a nation that defines itself through historical and continuing dispossession? This experience itself helps to explain precisely why place is so important in Scottish fiction. The invention of place is an act of re-possession. Places are not backdrops in Scottish fiction, they are statements, affirmations. Places assume the status of major characters, exerting their own wills and seeking their own destinies. Macdougall Hay's 'Brieston' is much more than a representation of the author's native Tarbert in *Gillespie* (1914), it is arguably the protagonist, the one character who will survive the despotic figure of Gillespie Strang. Such a place reaches beyond mere fact or fiction, it lodges deep in the national psyche.

All of this bypasses myopic kailyardisms, the only significance of which was the way it provoked writers to oppose it, and the way it coloured the popular reception of serious fiction. For 40 years, maybe more, from the 1890s onwards, fiction would be judged against the Maclarens and the Barries. This was not a matter of quality (how could it be?), but what became at issue were perceptions of local loyalty required by local readers. Kailyardism was safe. It did not disturb the peace. Its whimsy, its trite optimism, its insufferable moralising and its rancid sentimentality, all lent themselves to distorted notions of writerly virtue. Kailyardism became the model child telling the stories parents wanted to hear. They were the stories (remember Barrie's mother) the parents had told them in the first place. There is more than metaphorical significance in the fact that the first declared opponent of the kailyard, George Douglas Brown, was born illegitimate.

His mother was an Irish farm labourer. She gave him his father's full name, so he grew up as a walking accusation. There had been bastardy in Ochiltree and George Douglas Brown, senior, would never be allowed to forget it. And neither would the people of Ochiltree, so there was gossip. The sniping tongues of the 'bodies' in *The House With The Green Shutters* were drawn from the author's personal experience. After the death of his mother there was little left for him to betray in an Ochiltree he called 'Barbie'.

The novel was a revenge job, but it was the 'sentimental slop' of the Maclaren-Barrie school which was his target. The hypocrisy of kailyardism had personal significance for Brown. If his book made a parody of it, so did his life. Yes, he was a 'lad o' pairts', the dominie took an interest, the bursaries took him to Glasgow and Oxford Universities and he died at 32 of pneumonia. His masterpiece is an indictment against a vicious community, but it is more. Like Galt's best fiction, the novel portrays a local town caught between decay and progress. The railways come, the mines, the influx of Irish labours, new commercialism. Barbie is ripe for the coming man. The

Sir Compton Mackenzie at Drummond Place, Edinburgh, 1956.

*Alasdair Gray,
Liz Lochhead and
Edwin Morgan at
Glasgow Week in
Amsterdam, 1988.*

*A. J. Cronin and
family 'at home',
1938.*

decay is moral. It was a fictional town which provided a microcosm of mid-19th-century British community life.

Scotland was producing significant fiction at the rate of one novel every decade and a half: *Shutters* (1901), *Gillespie* (1914) and *Sunset Song* (1932). The period covered a world war, the Easter Rising, the Russian Revolution, Red Clydeside, the rise of Fascism in Italy, the General Strike, the Wall Street crash, the hunger marches, the election of a Labour Government in Britain and Hitler's seizure of power. The kailyard was still flourishing.

'Fathered between a kailyard and a bonny brier bush in the lee of a house with green shutters,' the new Minister says of Kinraddie. *Sunset Song* was to provide the classic example of local backlash in Scottish literary history.

When James Leslie Mitchell adopted his pseudonym to write it, when he changed the name of his boyhood croft from Bloomfield to Blawearie, and the neighbouring village from Arbuthnott to Kinraddie, it would have taken more than the old convention of fictionalising names to keep him out of trouble.

Allies might be hard won in nearby Drumlithie after Chris Guthrie's faithful reporting of, 'Folk said for a joke that every time it came on to rain the Drumlithie folk ran out and took in their steeple.' And Laurencekirk was mocked over its claim to have more right than Stonehaven to the status of county capital. The local newspaper which would have its say when the reviews came out, was ridiculed as 'The Squeeker'. There was logic behind this kind of procedure, operating on the principle that with the trading of insults it is best to be even-handed. Grassic Gibbon was nothing if not democratic in his treatment of the Mearns.

The reception for the novel grew lukewarm, then chilly, the closer it came from home. National reviewers praised it. 'The Squeeker' was a devotee of cabbages. Lost on Grassic Gibbon, apparently, was the beauty that is all around 'for him that has eyes to see it'. Moreover, it was a fault on his part to insist on calling a spade a spade 'when there is no need to mention that implement'. The newspaper issued the dark if hackneyed reminder: 'It's an ill bird that fouls its ain nest'.

Rob Middleton, the model for Long Rob in the novel, hugely enjoyed himself. 'You got me there,' he told the author. Less impressed was the author's mother. She disliked it, but took the precaution of being able to answer truthfully that she possessed copies of her son's books. They were wrapped up in brown paper and shelved in the kitchen press. Perhaps the most significant response was among those locals who seriously misunderstood the book. They were unable to grasp that it was fiction. They recognised it as an exercise in documentary reportage.

If this reaction affected Grassic Gibbon's confidence we can only look for evidence in the two novels, *Cloud Howe* (1933) and *Grey Granite* (1934), which completed the trilogy. The 'Segget' of *Cloud Howe* represented a compromise on the part of the author. Its carefully plotted location, between Arbuthnott and Laurencekirk, defied equation with any existing community. No such town existed, it was a pure composite. Similarly, the original 'Dundon' of *Grey Granite*, suggesting an Aberdeen/Dundee composite, was hastily revised by the author to 'Duncairn', and aspects of militant Glasgow, not to mention a Royal Mile, were thrown in. To add to the confusion, the 'Duncairn' which appeared in the earlier *Sunset Song*, where Chris attended school, was clearly identifiable with Stonehaven. The consequent blurring of focus, a city which conformed to the experience of no reader, did not aid the novel. This factor could be argued as at least contributing to the judgment that *Grey Granite* is the least successfully realised work in the trilogy.

J. M. Barrie,
Edinburgh, 1932.

*William McIlvanney
at Hampden Park,
Glasgow, 1988.*

This suggests an important rule: the Scottish writer may run personal risks if a fictional place is modelled too precisely on a real and familiar one, but the artistic risks involved in detaching or compositing that fictional place may be even more severe. It seems better to err on the side of local censure. It fades eventually, and is often wrong in any case.

This rule is certainly adopted by Scottish women writers. Catherine Carswell's *Open The Door* (1920) stripped bare genteel, middle-class Glasgow society. Her profiles of the immediate predecessors of Charles Rennie Mackintosh at Glasgow Art School resorted to only the thinnest of disguises, while Muriel Spark in *The Prime of Miss Jean Brodie* (1961) might have created a fictional Edinburgh school, the Marcia Blane School for Girls, but there is little impression here of deflecting attention from its prototype, the James Gillespie's School for Girls which the author attended, but of a sharpening of the social criticism. There is no nervous reticence in Spark's satire, but a universalism. Accentuation is the theme of the treatment of fictional places in the work of Scottish women writers. Willa Muir's Calderwick, in *Imagined Corners* (1931), portrays Montrose as a web of genteel hypocrisy, torn by sexual and religious conflicts. Nan Shepherd's Fetter-Rothnie, in *The Weatherhouse* (1930), based on an unspecified small community, one rooted clearly in a proximity to her native Aberdeen, may be a gentler, more sympathetic portrait, but few Scottish fictions have been so exact in their anatomisations of the social fabric of a community – in this case a society of girls, widows, wives and spinsters.

Another model is offered in the good fortune of John Galt, who discovered that even satire, or maybe particularly satire, can give rise to flattery. He based the 'Gudetown' of *The Provost* (1822) on his boyhood Irvine. His model for the self-interested, self-made, self-deluding narrator, Provost James Pawkie, was one Baillie Fullerton. Like Pawkie, Fullerton rose three times to become burgh provost and was mightily proud of the fact. Galt's background research on this consisted entirely of his memory of gossip heard as a boy. Three years after publication he was required to return to Irvine from London for the pleasant enough formality of receiving the freedom of the Royal Burgh. The dignitary who conferred the honour was the same Baillie Fullerton, inexplicably still alive and now in his 90s. After hearing the forgiving Baillie's speech, Galt recorded: 'Provost Pawkie himself could never have said anything half so good.' Was Pawkie an imitation of Fullerton, or Fullerton an imitation of Pawkie?

Fact or fiction, Scotland has been treated with considerably more accuracy and attention to detail by its own writers. Visiting authors consistently get the place wrong. Even temporary residence here has been known to drive imaginations wild. Alan Bold's *Scotland: A Literary Guide* (1989) is a valuable source on this disturbing trend. Mary Shelley spent two years in Broughty Ferry and never fully recovered. She wrote about the experience in the novel *Frankenstein* (1818). In her introduction to the 1831 edition of the novel she made the sad plea in mitigation: 'I lived principally in the country as a girl, and passed a considerable time in Scotland. I made occasional visits to the more picturesque parts; but my habitual residence was on the blank and dreary northern shores of the Tay, near Dundee.' Edgar Allan Poe never got round to explaining what effect an Irvine education had on his formative ideas, but clearly something very unhealthy happened to him somewhere along the line. George Orwell wrote *Nineteen Eighty-Four* on the island of Jura, and many consider the novel a very poor likeness.

James Leslie Mitchell, alias Lewis Grassic Gibbon, 1901-35.

JACK WEBSTER

A National Obsession

Scottish Football

TO THE EXTENT THAT AN OBSESSION MEANS YOU CAN THINK OF LITTLE else, it is an undeniable fact of life that the Scottish people have had an obsession with football down the generations.

As the sport grew out of the industrial working classes, it could perhaps be said that, sadly, there were many who had little else to think about. The weekend's respite from the depths and drudgery of the coal-mine or the sharp grind of the shipyard was to be found in the mellow glow of the pub and its contents and the emotional stirrings of the football ground. For there, on a Saturday afternoon, the cares of a world beset with poverty and depression could safely be shelved for two hours in favour of a spectacle of colour and masculine artistry which went some way to meeting the finer aspirations of ordinary folk.

They may never have seen a ballet or an opera in their lives but this was their artistic outlet, a means of satisfying the kind of inner need they probably wouldn't have stopped to identify. (How strange and wonderful that the beauty of football movement became so closely and popularly associated with the classical tones of Pavarotti's 'Nessun Dorma', as the musical theme of the 1990 World Cup in Italy.)

What's more, far from being the products of some alien class or culture, these performing footballers were recognisable neighbours, boys from the pit or steelyard who had learned their skills on the local cinder patch. In those inter-war years, it was the most commonplace experience to see hordes of men, from apprentice boys to middle-aged grandfathers, kicking a ball of sorts around a piece of wasteground. Disorganised scrambles, involving 30 or 40 aside, were the order of the day. It kept them fit and no doubt took minds off the bleakness of their prospects. It also fostered skills in those who had been blessed with a natural talent.

For those youngsters casting an eye on the impoverished existence of their elders, it also represented the biggest single hope of escape to a more congenial and lucrative way of life. Whole families like the Shanklys, whose backgrounds belonged to the pit-bings of Ayrshire, found new hope and prosperity in the playing and eventual management of football. The most famous member of the family, the redoubtable Bill, not only became a Scottish internationalist but converted Liverpool FC from mediocrity to the most distinguished team in England. Among his many utterings, he perhaps articulated beyond all others that Scottish obsession with the national sport when he once declared: 'No no, football is not a matter of life or death. It's far more important than that!'

Out of that same coal-mining mould as the Shanklys came the most influential man that Scottish football has ever known, the legendary Jock Stein from Burnbank, Hamilton. Stein was never a star performer on the field of play (seven of his prime years spent with Albion Rovers hardly presaged greatness), but his mastery of technique, plus a developing talent for bringing the best out of the human condition, belatedly turned him into the game's most significant figure of the 20th century.

Pavarotti arrives at Prestwick Airport, 1990.

Street football.

Bill Shankly in action, England versus Scotland, 1938.

Rescued from the obscurity of Welsh non-league football towards the end of his playing career, merely to help a struggling Celtic FC in an emergency, Jock Stein galvanised the team to a League-and-Cup double in 1954. It was just the beginning of a remarkable career. Taking charge of the Celtic boys in the late 1950s, he then went off to manage Dunfermline and Hibernian but returned to Parkhead in 1965, in time to reap the harvest of his earlier labours.

By 1967, he had moulded a team of home-grown youngsters into the most successful club side that Scotland had ever seen, carrying off the European Cup and giving his local heroes the title of Lisbon Lions. They were the first British team to win the top honour in Europe, paving the way for English victories thereafter, and the feat has yet to be emulated by any other Scottish side.

Under the influence of Stein's genius, Celtic chalked up an incredible nine Scottish League victories in a row and, in 1970, failed only at the final hurdle of yet another European Cup triumph. Rangers reacted by signing seven or eight of Scotland's best players, a panic measure which failed to dent the Celtic supremacy, while denuding other Scottish clubs of their best players, but at least it brought the consolation of the European Cup Winners' Cup of 1972.

Subsequently, Jock Stein was lucky to survive a horrendous car crash on the A74 but was never the same force again. He eventually stepped aside at Celtic Park (in favour of his Lisbon Lions' captain, Billy McNeill) but revived sufficiently to become Scotland's manager for the World Cup campaigns of 1982 and 1986. In the very hour of qualifying for the latter, he collapsed and died of a heart attack, a tragic and dramatic end for a man who had given his life to football.

To men like Stein and Shankly and many others, football had indeed been a life-long obsession, a feeling heightened in the West of Scotland in particular by the on-going rivalry of Rangers and Celtic. The purely sporting connotation of that rivalry had long been muddied by religious undertones, Rangers representing the Protestant side, and Celtic, the Roman Catholic.

Rangers had been under fire for the unexplained absence of Roman Catholics on the Ibrox playing staff, a situation which went far beyond the bounds of coincidence, despite periodic statements that no sectarian policy existed within the club. The matter was finally resolved in 1989 when the Ibrox club, by then under the new management of businessman David Murray as chairman, and Graeme Souness as team boss, embraced a Roman Catholic in the most dramatic fashion. Their signing of Maurice Johnston was a controversial matter not only because he was a Catholic but because he had already been a Celtic player and was on the point of joining the club once more. His first appearance in a Rangers jersey at Parkhead brought the kind of reception that might have greeted the Devil on applying for a senior post in the Vatican. By switching camps, Johnston had guaranteed as much opposition from the Catholic community as he would receive from a minority of Rangers' supporters, to whom any contact with the other side was akin to flirting with leprosy.

Celtic, on the other hand, had pursued the not-uncommon Catholic route of pragmatism, taking advantage of whatever forces might further their cause, irrespective of religious background. Indeed, their greatest legend, Jock Stein, had been firmly associated with the Protestant cause. But if harnessing the opposition could bear you to the heights of European glory, then what the hell?

The Rangers-Celtic issue to some extent reflected the situation in Northern

Craig Levein of Hearts in action versus Hibs, Edinburgh, 1989.

*Graeme Souness
and Walter Smith at
Ibrox, 1986.*

*Maurice Johnston
in action against
Yugoslavia at
Hampden Park,
1988.*

Ireland, though mercifully the violence of that unfortunate country had failed to reach the streets of Glasgow. Clashes between the rival supporters had been confined to fleeting battles in the aftermath of matches, the worst outbreak in modern times having taken place across the pitch at Hampden in the Scottish Cup final of 1980.

Meanwhile, the rest of Scotland has looked upon the Rangers-Celtic rivalry with little sympathy, more concerned about the fact that the wealth and intimidating power of the two Glasgow clubs have so dominated Scottish football throughout the century as to render the situation close to farce. When you consider that, in the 43 years from 1904 to 1947, the Scottish League Championship was won by Motherwell in 1931 and on every other occasion by either Rangers or Celtic, it does raise the valid question of what role the other teams in Scotland could possibly have been playing, except that of cannon fodder.

Such imbalance of power within a small country like Scotland does present a very real problem, one not experienced in England, where any one of ten clubs has either the money or support, or both, to challenge the kind of monopoly that has become known as the Old Firm in Scotland. There was no easy answer to the Scottish farce and it might well have continued without interruption except for a chain of events which started with St Mirren sacking their manager, Alex Ferguson, in 1978. That, by chance, took place in the same week as Billy McNeill had been called home to Celtic Park to succeed Jock Stein, having just cut his managerial teeth with a year as boss of Aberdeen. Now searching for a manager, the Pittodrie directors decided that the man no longer wanted at Paisley might well be the answer to their dilemma.

Their judgement could not have been more inspired. Alex Ferguson, himself a former Rangers player, so challenged the supremacy of Rangers and Celtic as to crack the mould of their monopoly and put Aberdeen into a golden age of its own. In the first seven seasons of the 1980s, the Dons of Pittodrie won the Premier Division Championship three times, the Scottish Cup four times and topped it all by carving their way to the top of the continental scene and winning the European Cup Winners' Cup of 1983, beating the legendary Real Madrid in the Gothenburg final. Crowning that with a victory over the 1983 European Cup winner, Hamburg, the Aberdonians confirmed themselves as not only the top team in Scotland but in Europe as well. More significantly perhaps, they had raised the sights of other teams in the country, showing what could be done when you set aside the inferiority complex which developed over years of being . . . well, inferior.

Under manager Jim McLean, Dundee United took up the message and followed Aberdeen to their own first-ever League Championship. They, too, aspired to the heights of Europe and failed only at the hurdle of a UEFA Cup final. So long starved of fresh angles to the story of Scottish football, the headline writers gladly latched on to the notion that a 'New Firm' of Aberdeen and Dundee United had taken over from the Old Firm of Rangers and Celtic.

That bid for geographic balance was further aided when yet another East Coast club, Heart of Midlothian, long separated from its glamour days of a previous generation but now inspired by the entrepreneurial leadership of property man Wallace Mercer, came close to joining the New Firm.

Whether or not this new challenge sprang from the tighter concentration of a ten-club Premier Division will remain a matter for argument. But the outcome did inspire a broader interest in the game, around parts of

*The triumphant
Rangers bring the
European Cup
Winners' Cup back
to Ibrox, Glasgow,
1972.*

*The victorious Celts
arrive at Paradise,
Glasgow, 1967.*

*Billy McNeill and
assistant Tommy
Craig celebrate
against Dundee
United, 1988.*

*Celtic fans celebrate
the club's European
triumph, George
Square, Glasgow,
1967.*

*Celtic fans return
from Lisbon in
celebratory mood,
Abbotsinch Airport,
Glasgow, 1967.*

*Alex Ferguson
watches his Scotland
squad at Girvan,
1986.*

Dundee United players lift manager Jim McLean after winning the Premier League, Dundee, 1983.

A joyous Aberdeen bench at Gothenburg, 1983.

*A minibus of
Rangers fans leave
for Barcelona,
Glasgow, 1972.*

Scotland where they had long since resigned themselves to playing inferior fiddles.

The history of Scottish football will show that the New Firm dominance slipped in the later 1980s, when its architect, Alex Ferguson, went off to manage Manchester United and Rangers came under the control of Scotland's most successful young businessman, David Murray, a son of Ayr and creator of Murray International Metals.

The business shrewdness of Murray not only expanded the Ibrox club to a commercial enterprise far beyond the field of play; it geared its football efforts, thus backed by spectacular funding, towards a new concept of European participation. Whatever shape that might eventually take, if the richest clubs in Europe were planning a destiny of their own, then Murray was determined that Rangers would be up there fighting. His spending of vast millions on highly rated talents gave warning of his intentions, even if his signing of one half of England's international team raised dilemmas among those dyed-in-the-wool Scots who thought all Englishmen were bastards!

The fresh fortunes of Rangers were by no means matched at Celtic Park, where the team ran into the bleakness of 1989/90, when they won only ten of their 36 league matches. So the burning resentment of Glasgow's East End demanded new effort from a board which seemed sluggish and unimaginative. Now it would be Celtic's turn to fight back, just as it had been Rangers' turn 20 years earlier.

All this concentration on club fortunes, much stimulated by European competition, had quietly been eroding the general interest in the Scottish national team. Oh, there was still a fascination about doing unkind things to the English and the forays into World Cup contest every four years were guaranteed to raise enthusiasm. But gone were the days when any appearance of a Scottish team would bring out large crowds to Hampden Park. In keeping with a more widespread modern obsession, any game which did not have a competitive meaning was likely to appeal to no more than 25,000 people in the 1990s, compared to many times that number a generation earlier.

In those post-war years, when Hampden held upwards of 135,000, there had still been countless thousands unable to get tickets. That brings us to a conclusion that the old obsession with football is not what it used to be. Of course there is still a fiercely committed interest in pockets like Ibrox and Parkhead and sound displays of loyalty across the rest of Scotland. But the obsession has undoubtedly diminished, in tandem with the old definition of poverty. The rising affluence of the post-war years has turned the population to a vast new range of leisure pursuits, where participation has replaced the mere spectating. It is hard to argue with the good sense of that. Little boys will even play with their home computers rather than kick a tanner ba' against a tenement wall. Indeed the streets of Scotland, once filled with the budding Patsy Gallachers and Jimmy Johnstones, Alan Mortons and Willie Hendersons, are strangely empty these days.

That stage of social development has passed to the economically poorer

A Scotland versus England crowd, Hampden Park, Glasgow, 1968.

countries which began to show their skills in the World Cup finals of 1990. It all takes us back to the root of how the game of football tends to work its way through a social system. (The exception of West Germany to the social theory owes much to the character and disciplined strengths of that nation.)

If the passion is not what it used to be, you can bet there are consolations. Frankly, in an age of materialism and greater sophistication, there are things which are more important. For one thing, the wider spectrum of the arts is more readily available to the general public. It may be hard to swallow that there are erstwhile football fans now watching orchestral concerts, ballet and opera, as well as sampling golf, squash, bowls, curling, sailing and a dozen other pursuits. But it is a fact of life, even if it will never stop old men dreaming about the silken soccer-skills of a bygone day. The grand old game will always be with us. I think we are merely getting it into better perspective.

Jock Stein moves the goalposts with Andy Roxburgh, Largs, 1978.

MURRAY RITCHIE

Folkies

Modern Scottish Folk Music

FOLK MUSIC IS CULTURE AT ITS LEAST SOPHISTICATED, ENTERTAINMENT at its most simple, which is why it is the most abused and plundered of all the arts. Just as running is the most natural of all sports, folk songs are the starting point for all artistic performance. Pete Seeger, the American father figure of folk, who made his name singing the songs of his country until they were 'discovered' by recording companies and converted into currency, complained: 'Big business changed the nature of folk music. There was always some guy around to commercialise it if there was a dollar to be turned.'

Nowadays folk is less fashionable than it was in the 1950s and 1960s but it continues to thrive in a natural and healthy state without being force-fed by the demands of commerce. In Scotland the folk tradition is glorious but it has had to overcome a more difficult obstacle than mere commercialism on the journey from its very varied roots to the folk revival of the 1950s when the Scottish people began to rediscover the wonder and wealth of their own musical history and culture.

Like much of Scottish art Scotland's folk tradition had come to be regarded as a discredited sub-culture. Very few folk songs were sung or taught in Scottish schools. A few Burnsian drawing-room ballads were about the extent of the average Scottish child's education in Scottish folk music. Questions about Scottish poetry and music in examination papers were purely token. Like so much of Scottish art and culture, folk music was left to rot and to be forgotten, just another victim of the conspiracy to disdain all things distinctively un-British after the Treaty of Union.

In my youth in Dumfries (where I was baptised in St Michael's Church, in which Burns worshipped and in whose kirkyard he is buried) I was once told in all seriousness by a respected local man of letters that Burns was really rather second-rate because his poetry did not scan as well as that of English poets. This chap was no Anglophile, merely one who, typically, had been brought up to believe in the essential inferiority of Scottish artistic expression and our inevitable failure to withstand comparison with English culture. There were many like him, even in the very town where Burns was recognised and revered for the genius he was when he lived and worked there.

It took a big rehabilitation job by the giants of the Scottish cultural renaissance to reverse this insidious and effective onslaught on Scottish culture. The greatest of all was, of course, Hugh MacDiarmid, another Dumfriesshire poet who complained that in Scotland we ignored Burns's poetry while preserving his furniture. He was right on that point without question, but only for a time. Yet even MacDiarmid, the lifelong champion of Scottish culture, stopped short of embracing the folk tradition in all respects. He took the arrogant view of the hectoring intellectual, denouncing traditional singing as the 'ranting of illiterates'. He despised poetry which did not come moulded and refined by years of literary research and education. He said that Hebridean singers of Gaelic songs sounded like seagulls. Yet this was the same MacDiarmid who attacked Received Pronunciation in

A man of his time in music hall, Harry Lauder, 1870-1950.

spoken English and denounced the paucity of passion in English poetry while speaking up for the Glasgow accent because of its proletarian authenticity.

Many respected and dedicated people, not least Sir Walter Scott, recognised the treasure house of music and song which existed in the disparate cultures of Scotland before it began to rot after the Union. Scott especially made a point of collecting songs. In his classic *Minstrelsy of the Scottish Border* he talked of the passionate addiction to music of the Scots and their kindred Celts in Ireland and Wales much of which was being saved by the spread of the printing press. Scott noted: 'Some persons seem to have had what their contemporaries probably thought the bizarre taste of gathering and preserving collections of this fugitive poetry.'

Gavin Greig, the Aberdeenshire schoolmaster, was another who compiled a magnificent collection of these 'fugitive' songs rich enough to withstand comparison with any in the world. In the early years of this century Greig, with the help of a North-East minister, the Rev. James B. Duncan of Lynturk, set out to preserve in print the wealth of material known only to the oral tradition. Nightly, Greig cycled from his school house at Whitehill of New Deer, to scour Buchan, noting words and music from old people whose sources stretched back to the 18th-century and post-Culloden Scotland. A brilliant musician himself, (distantly related to Edvard Grieg, the Norwegian composer of Scots descent), Greig would sit at a roadend somewhere, often in foul weather, coaxing half-forgotten verses from his friends and noting them by lantern-light. Greig and Duncan ended up with 3,500 folk songs and 3,300 different tunes. Greig died prematurely at the outbreak of the First World War. The remarkable feat of Greig and Duncan is only now in the late 20th century, being published in book form – eight substantial volumes – by Aberdeen University together with the School of Scottish Studies in Edinburgh.

Another of the great historians of Scottish folk music, Hamish Henderson, of the School of Scottish Studies, is a socialist republican, poet and song writer. He believes folk music will never die, despite political fashion and the recent loss of impetus which the radicals gave the revival in the 1950s and 1960s. Where Greig and Burns and Scott traipsed around the countryside jotting down songs and snatches, Henderson would be found in some tinker's tent with a tape recorder.

Like Scott, Burns collected and rewrote many 'fugitive' songs and poems, sometimes to make bawdy ditties respectable, sometimes to make them even more ribald. His *Merry Muses of Caledonia* is a record of his interest in bawdy song. Music at the disposal of the successive collectors presented a rich variety, from Gaelic mouth-music to Jacobite rebel songs, from the cornkisters and bothy ballads of the North-East to the Border ballads of reiving and warring with England, from straightforward love songs to the gallus street songs of Glasgow and the cities, from the work songs of fishermen and farmers to the newer songs of the industrial era's coal miners, railwaymen and shipbuilders. Very few nations in Europe could offer such a range of contrasts and styles, and very few nations had it suppressed in the way that Scotland's frequently seditious music was put down; not so much by the brute force which came after the failure of the '45 Rebellion but by the unspoken, Anglocentric approach to culture which ensured that anything in the way of defiance or any verse expressive of national sentiment was to be deplored not just as subversive but as second rate and culturally demeaning.

There was, indeed, sedition in the Jacobite airs like the 'Wee, Wee German Lairdie' which were all but lost for a time:

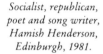

FOLKIES

110

Socialist, republican, poet and song writer, Hamish Henderson, Edinburgh, 1981.

Auld Scotland, thou'rt ower cauld a hole
For nursin' sicca vermin
But the very dogs of England's court
They bark and howl in German.

Ignoring inconvenient sentiment of this kind in the hope that it would go away was understandable in a way. Scotland had been dragged against the wishes of its people into Union with England, and Burns was typical of the Scots who were outraged by the betrayal of their sovereignty and their nation's independence: the blistering contempt of 'A Parcel o' Rogues in a Nation' was one of his responses. For folk music has always contained the unrestrained expression of the people's dissent: it is the natural medium of those with no power except the power to ridicule authority or attack it in verse and song. Kings and politicians were not the only objects of derision by the people. Hardship in the days before and during the industrial revolution provided incentive for ordinary people to inveigh against anyone who made life even more intolerable. Burns, as usual, spoke for everyone against life's oppressions: in 'The Quodlibet' he wrote:

A fig for those by law protected,
Liberty's a glorious feast.
Courts for cowards were erected,
Churches built to please the priest.

If some of Burns's work and all of the Jacobite songs were laden with fine sedition and protest, the ballads of the North-East offered not just fun and expressions of love for bonnie lasses, but broadsides against miserable landowners. Border songs frequently expressed nationalism, not of the counterfeit sort which nowadays has become associated with the bogus Brigadoon type of embarrassing music-hall Scottishness, but of a simple love for the country and its people.

All of this culture was effectively crushed for a long time. The Gael's way of life was, of course, crushed by force along with the wearing of tartan. Much of what was left was crushed by Scotland's involuntary cultural assimilation with England. Two world wars in the first part of the 20th century reinforced the 'Britishness' of this unnatural cultural merger. Scottishness in culture was mostly discredited and consigned to music hall. Sir Harry Lauder was very much a man of his time in music hall, one who came to typify this imaginary Scotland to the amusement of the English and the embarrassment of Scots who resented their culture being distorted into the 'Stop Yer Tickling, Jock' formula. Or perhaps the Scots were by now too brainwashed to know the difference. Sir Harry Lauder was, after all, hugely popular in Scotland where he turned Scots into figures of ridicule. Pete Seeger's point about commercial exploitation was never more apt than in Scotland.

Not until after two world wars had been fought did this diminution of Scotland's cultural distinctiveness begin to be re-examined. Although the wars united the Scots and English in the name of survival, there seems little question now that the role of the Scots regiments reinforced in the Scots an awareness of their own national identity. In a curious way the Jocks who piped British troops into battle and gave them their best marching and fighting tunes were never anything but Scots. Indeed it was pride in their Scottishness which fuelled their famous ferocity in battle. The end of war presaged the end of Empire, and the political dependency culture which

FOLKIES

112

*Police carry
an anti-Polaris
demonstrator off the
depot ship* Proteus *in
the Holy Loch.*

had been piledriven into Scotland began to wane. When the generation of war babies grew up to enjoy the fruits of education for all in Scotland, the perception of being Scottish as well as (or instead of) British began to spread.

MacDiarmid's lifelong dedication to reinvigorating Scottish culture now began to show results. The old radicalism of the Scots reasserted itself and in the dying years of the Macmillan era of British politics (Macmillan was typical of the anglicised Scot who referred habitually to Britain as England) the folk revival exploded throughout Scotland – and England, too. Many social trends encouraged this cultural phenomenon. In 1951 a group of nationalists stole the Stone of Destiny from Westminster Abbey, a crime (or act of patriotism, depending on your view) which delighted all Scotland, earning the disapproval of only the Establishment of the day. That symbolic deed, which ended with the stone being returned – and it *was* returned, despite mischievous suggestions to the contrary – inspired many rebel songs which three decades later have become part of the folk tradition. The Coronation itself enraged many Scots who did not want the Queen known as Elizabeth II because there had never been an Elizabeth I of Scotland. A few pillar boxes were dynamited in support of nationalism and some of those responsible now sit in fine company, their guilty secrets of youthful adventure safe for life.

The late Thurso Berwick (the republican, nationalist schoolteacher, Morris Blythman) had a knack for poetically articulating working-class popular sentiment. He wrote in the chorus of 'The Scottish Breakaway':

> Nae Liz the Twa,
> Nae Lillibet the Wan,
> Nae Liz will ever dae,
> For we'll mak' oor land republican
> In a Scottish breakaway . . .

Blythman was a powerful force in the folk revival, writing songs which touched the exposed nerve of Scottish consciousness in the 1950s. His work was noted for its Glasgow wit and devilment and owed some of its popularity

Robin Hall and Jimmy Macgregor entertain at the Safari Park, Blair Drummond, 1974.

*Andy Stewart at the
Xmas show, Kings
Theatre, Edinburgh,
1960.*

to his clever idea of putting his subversive lyrics to the familiar tunes of the Orange movement. 'The Scottish Breakaway' was sung to the tune of 'The Sash My Father Wore' which is the divisive anthem of religious bigotry but is also, in truth, an Irish folk song. Either way it commended itself to all ordinary people. In those days the notions of republicanism, nationalism and good old-fashioned Clydeside socialism were strong, if mostly confined to the populous West of Scotland where economic oppression was most felt, but it was largely ignored by press and television. Only the folk-music circuit, some of it underground, gave it an outlet, providing a release for the pressure. Folk music, forever the voice of the people, became a vehicle for their protest at the arrival of American nuclear naval forces in the Clyde. Immediately a host of protest songs, many of them witty and appealing to young people awakening to their new importance to public opinion, became popular – and at their root they had the idea of a radical, disrespectful, reawakening Scottishness.

> Forget the old Orange and Green,
> Forget the old Orange and Green,
> Let's put all our hate
> On that Sassenach State,
> Forget the old Orange and Green.

By injecting radical politics into folk music the revivalists of the 1950s and 1960s attracted the interest of the young generation whose curiosity led them to rediscover their folk heritage. One huge benefit brought about by this process was the first resistance by public opinion to the television-sponsored abuse of Scottish culture. That era was the beginning of the end for the make-believe culture of haggis and heather, buts and bens and fairy glens, a mawkish distortion which had bedevilled Scottish musical culture for a century. In his book, *101 Scottish Songs*, Norman Buchan MP, another collector, song-writer and champion of political protest, condemned this trend as 'kailyairdery':

> Not a glen but it has its but and ben. Not a granny but she is old and frail and we have to be kind to her. And what a waving of tartan around the heiland hames, ain wee hooses, stars o' Rabbie Burns. We cannot help but feel that the Glasgow street cry, "ye canny shove yer granny aff a bus" has more of truth and reality than the slobbering over her in a distant and imaginary hieland hame.

While the revival was in full swing some folk singers became television stars. Robin Hall (one of whose schoolteachers was Morris Blythman) and Jimmie Macgregor, the outstanding folk performers of the time, commanded handsome salaries for appearing nightly on popular networked BBC programmes (and were denounced by the Tory *Sunday Express* for wearing CND badges). In Scotland there were programmes like *Hootenannie* and *Jig Time* on Scottish TV in which folk singers became household names. The late Josh MacRae sang with a group called the Reivers and by himself had at least one record in the hit parade.

Josh MacRae gave many people of the time an abiding interest in folk music. In a crumbling, rat-infested Labour club in Dumfries, he appeared one night in the early 1960s in support of a by-election candidate. For my sins I had written a story in the local paper referring to Andy Stewart as a 'folk singer' and MacRae's friends were not slow to point out that this was an appalling inaccuracy. Of course, the truth was that Andy Stewart

Dougie McLean with his wife Jennifer, 1989.

Dick Gaughan,
1983.

was seen by most Scots in those days as a folk singer of sorts: that was the extent of the dismissal of our genuine folk heritage. (I do not seek to discredit a popular comedian and performer, but folk singer Mr Stewart was not.) MacRae's performance was memorable enough to give me a lifelong love of folk music in many forms and there were others like him. Some, like MacRae himself, fell victim to a fashionably self-destructive lifestyle. He sang rebel songs, nationalist songs, socialist songs and republican songs, many of them introduced with the advice that they were already proscribed, which added to their fascination. (Many were censored by the BBC.)

By that time, the Left in Scotland had effectively hijacked the folk revival, turning the folk tradition into a vehicle for protest and political crusading. Those days are passing which perhaps explains why folk music today is perhaps less politically-charged than it once was and why it remains – as ever – popular with people of all views whose first love is the music and whose radicalism is no longer taken for granted. At the same time pop music has taken on a new meaning for younger people, particularly in Scotland, where groups now openly denounce the political establishment of Scotland and for their trouble become vilified by reactionary politicians. It would, of course, be a disaster if some politicians were to praise them. Folk music, like pop, has never been at its most robust when patronised.

Today's folk scene is as diverse and fertile as it ever was with traditionalists and modern solo singer-songwriters drawing crowds, and noisy folk-pop bands such as Runrig and the Dougie McLean Band winning loyal followings. Who can explain the phenomenon which takes place regularly in Glasgow where in one well-known club they have to turn away dozens of people wanting into a ceilidh (and them not even Gaelic speakers)? And why do young people who have never heard of Josh MacRae now turn up to hear songs which are centuries old and others which were written in the folk tradition yesterday? Or turn out on miserable winter evenings to fill halls listening to groups like the Whistlebinkies or to singers like Dick Gaughan whose driving guitar and rasping delivery pour out defiance and outrage, just as the songs of centuries ago did for his countrymen? It is because young people are enjoying their first natural contact with the arts and discovering their own culture.

At the risk of oversimplifying the argument, it must be obvious that the Scots and their centuries of tradition and musical culture cannot easily be separated. The enemies of Scottish culture have tried force; they have tried ignoring our tradition; they have tried proscribing it by censorship (the BBC in Scotland had a lot to answer for in this respect in the 1960s just as the Scottish press had a lot to answer for in respect of MacDiarmid during much of his life until he became old and regarded, therefore, as no longer dangerously radical). Scots remain closer to their music than most other cultures, just as Scott observed in his day more than a century ago. This is probably why they care too much to agree on their own national anthem.

But mainly, folk music survives because it is fun. In folk clubs throughout Scotland the traditional songs are nightly supplemented by contemporary writing which in time passes into the folk tradition. Without that steady contribution of fresh material folk music would atrophy. But it never does. It is always first to comment on social events, whether wars, elections, coronations, scandals. It is always the first medium of complaint, the first voice of delight or love. It can be messed about, commercialised, exploited, debased but never silenced.

*Seaweed-eating
Orkney sheep,
1974.*

JIM HEWITSON

The Margin of Scotland
The Island of Papa Westray

IT'S LATE ON A LUMINOUS NORTHERN EVENING. DOWN BY THE PIER WHERE the basin is being deepened three old men lean on the railing and gaze, misty-eyed, across the bay. Yet another soul-stirring Orkney sunset burnishes the horizon in a coloursplash of gold, crimson and orange. It's the sort of skyscape folk travel from the other side of the world to view.

'Boys, boys, wid ye look at that,' says the first veteran in awe.

'Magnificent,' says the second.

'Aye,' says the third, 'finest bit o' dredging equipment we've had here in 20 years.'

The English journalist who collected this anecdote retells it with relish. It seems that the media fascination with our Scottish islands and their curious inhabitants is insatiable.

Although he probably doesn't know it, our newsman's tale, apocryphal or not, is important because it operates at more than one level. As well as being a couthy yarn it illustrates a startling metamorphosis overtaking these northern isles, perhaps the single biggest change since the Crofters Commission sailed through the archipelago in the 1880s and helped bring the ordinary folk out of centuries of agricultural servitude.

The natural splendours of Orkney, taken for granted since the days when Magnus Barelegs was a boy, now hold the key to the area's future prosperity. Tourism is catching up with fishing and farming as a principal money-earner but only recently have the folk come to appreciate that the golden sunsets can be translated into hard cash. Small islands with their unusual appeal are now big business.

For the past few years the far-flung northern isles of Orkney have been my base of operation yet I feel drawn from time to time back to my roots beside the Clyde; my anchor drags, as it has done in Edinburgh, Umbria and Athens, on a restless tide which ebbs and flows between nostalgia and novelty.

Private pilgrimages can take many contrasting forms. Venturing south I always pay my respects at my childhood home – one of the few Clydebank tenements to have survived the hammer of the demolisher who in the past 20 years has sent the great, grey buildings tumbling in a way even the Luftwaffe failed to do.

The second stage on this spiritual journey draws me inevitably to an unremarkable side room in the National Museum of Antiquities in Edinburgh, packed with Pictish symbol stones and incised sandstone from Scotland's Dark Ages. Here I can view a cross-slab from the kirk of St Boniface on Papa Westray – now my island home. This part of the pilgrimage usually comes towards the end of my stay in the South when, in the midst of the scurry of the city, I need a sight of durable lifeline to a place where events progress at a more sensible pace.

Papa Westray, or Papay as it is styled by the local folk, can at times seem impossibly far away. When you're queuing for a ticket amidst the throng at Queen Street station or fighting to order a round in one or other of the howffs down Fleshmarket Close our isle can seem about as real as the fantastic, fogbound Orcadian kingdom of Hether Blether.

My first visit to that sanctuary of venerable stones in Edinburgh, to firm up my new northern connections, gave me much food for thought. I found our Papay cross-slab nicely displayed among its cold expressionless companions but to my confusion discovered that the large wall-chart of Scotland not only failed to pinpoint the St Boniface site but also appeared to have allowed Papa Westray to slip beneath the waves.

I suspect that our scatter of islands have been as much trouble to the map makers over the years as they have been to the long line of Scottish kings who have tried to keep these distant, independently-minded territories under their sway. Cartographers always seemed to have it in for Orkney and Shetland in particular, dropping them into waterproof boxes somewhere east of Aberdeen or Dundee – mysterious floating archipelagos existing on the boundaries of reality.

In a sense I think this is often how the rest of the United Kingdom looks on Scotland's island fringe, romantic, scenically attractive yet somehow unconnected with the greater life of Scotland – the soft outer edge. Of course, nothing could be further from the truth since some of the most exciting initiatives of the past decade have come from these peripheral areas with co-operative enterprises, educational developments such as distance learning, fish farming, arts and music festivals and many pioneering tourist projects.

But how did this strange island fever overtake a level-headed boy from the sandstone canyons of Clydebank where the nearest we have to sceptred isles in the vicinity of Kilbowie Road are the upturned supermarket trolleys in the ponds which formed stretches of the once splendid Forth and Clyde Canal – the Nolly? Summer holidays spent in the 1950s at North Berwick were, I think, the source of the obsession. A little way along the coast towards Gullane is Fidra, a lump of rock which I was later told was the inspiration for Robert Louis Stevenson's *Treasure Island*. Building sandcastles at Yellowcraig I would look out over the surf towards this little volcanic stump, the haunt of seabirds and holy men, so close to shore yet so tantalisingly far away; like looking at another world through a half-open door.

For me Stevenson's book has always conjured images of a palm-shrouded tropical isle with sweeping sandy bays and dark jungle glades where one-eyed pirates lurk behind every tree trunk; as different as could be from the windy outcrop with its lighthouse in the Firth of Forth. Yet Fidra remained mysterious and compelling. I did eventually visit and there was no sense of let-down. It was a kingdom waiting to be ruled, a private paradise. It may have commenced as childish fancy but I was hooked.

As the years moved on I developed similar attachments to the beautiful islands of Loch Lomond, to the Bass Rock and to Inchmahome on the Lake of Menteith where green lawns reach for lapping waters in the shadow of the tumbled priory walls.

This location provides the best illustration I know of the phenomenon of islands in aspic, places frozen in time like St Kilda and Fidra. They are beautiful certainly, spiritually uplifting perhaps, but they lack the people, the society, no matter how small, to breathe life into their empty acres. On the other hand we find Papa Westray and islands like Foula, Fair Isle, Colonsay and Coll. They may also be small (four square miles in Papa Westray's case) but they have genuine communities, a world in miniature with all the consequent joys and kindnesses, petty jealousy and bloody-mindedness.

Kelp-burning in the Orkney Isles, 1933.

They are not perfect, paradise they are not, but in their struggle through each day they are vibrant, decidedly alive.

Papa Westray's population is small – around 80 when the children are home from the hostel in Kirkwall – and naturally there are strong family ties among the Rendalls, Cursiters, Davidsons etc. Almost everyone on the island seems to be related to their neighbours, second cousins and school-age aunties and uncles abound; there's a wealth of island folklore and local history lives to such an eerie extent that events of 100 years ago are spoken of as if they had happened only yesterday. The island has a rich, if small-scale, heritage of fishing and farming and if the new money spinner, tourism, can be successfully grafted on to this mini-economy then the future is bright.

Around Scotland there are said to be as many islands as there are days of the year (Hether Blether appears in a Leap Year, of course). Although they have many features in common each island has a distinctive personality and special qualities. For example Papa Westray is a place where the five senses, dulled or damaged by the clamour of urban living, can be restored to full vigour. Let's explore a little.

Just LISTEN to the groan of the *Islander*'s mooring ropes as she strains to be away from the New Pier on her three-hour journey to Kirkwall; the chug of Tommy o' Maybo's ancient tractor as he climbs the brae to the shop; the screech of the Arctic terns beyond Sheepheight as they divebomb the foolhardy backpacker; the excited shouts of the five children in the schoolyard; the lark concluding his symphony above the boat masts at Skennist; the throaty roar as the afternoon flight from Kirkwall turns on the tarmac in front of the one-room terminal; the haunting sound of the seals calling across on the Holm; the bleet of the new-born lamb or the last shallow breath of the old ewe.

Or LOOK for the aquamarine transparency of the South Wick, with water so clear you can count the partans crawling across the seabed, 20 feet below the keel; kittiwakes and razorbills diving and carousing under the formidable, overhanging cliffs at the north end; weather fronts fast approaching, great battlements of cloud rolling in from the West; lights twinkling on the fishing boats in the Sound as they head north for Fair Isle; the high jinks of the kittens in the yard chasing a Red Admiral; the co-op bus with its daily cargo of wide-eyed tourists and the huge winter seas smashing into the geos on the west shore, their journey across the Atlantic complete.

And SMELL the pungent odour of the kelp piled six-feet-high along the shore, torn last month from its watery bed by the fiercest of seas; the distinctive aroma of freshly caught crab or lobster boiling in the pot; the new mown hay; the sweet scent of the carpet of wildflowers at Moclett and the breathtaking bouquet of Bill o' Links home brew after the thunder has got to it.

Then FEEL the blown hay itching your back midway through a warm afternoon at the baling; the creel rope opening the blisters on your fingers as you haul out beyond Weelie's Taing; the soft, warm down of the wayward snipe chick as you return him to the nest or the smooth perfection of the stonework at the farmstead at the Knap of Howar – built before the mighty pyramids.

Or TASTE the island delicacy of clapshot (a mash of tatties and neeps) and the salty flavour of the Holmie mutton at the Muckle Supper; Mima of Cott's flavoursome duff; the clean, wholesome tang of the whelks gathered below the Old Mill and the silky, deceptive quality of Peter Miller's rhubarb wine which has graced many a shindig.

*Hurricane damage
in the Orkney Isles,
1952.*

*Seals on North
Ronaldsay, 1983.*

Around this framework of the senses a new Papa Westray is being constructed – one which hopefully will never be forced down the sorrowful road followed by others around the island fringe to gradual depopulation and eventual desertion.

Although visitors to Orkney may find the abandoned, desert islands with their roofless crofts, rusting farm equipment and tumbledown jetty atmospheric, I find them infinitely sad. They have become like Inchmahome, beautiful but empty, so empty. The wind cries out for the generations who once brought life to the hearth and shore. They are a sad legacy of communities who failed to cope with the pressures of the 20th century when the just demands of the younger folk for a less severe lifestyle could often only be met across the water.

Two factors have combined as the century draws to a close and have turned this situation on its head. The first is tourism and the second, the influx of settlers from the South – the quiet invasion.

Gone are the days on Papa Westray when teams of oxen worked the fields, the fishing fleet went out in strength, kelp was big business and the population could be numbered in hundreds. While the traditional industries still hold sway the tourist trade now touches most families on the island. The guest house and hostel run by our community co-operative and established with help from the Highlands and Islands Development Board now greets visitors from five continents during our short but spectacular summer.

At this crossroads several schools of thought meet. There are people on the island convinced we should go flat out to exploit the boom while it lasts, an unashamed open-door policy; others argue that with increased leisure time tourism will grow steadily and call for phased development to protect the special social and physical environment; there are others who simply get on with the work around the farm and wonder what all the fuss is about.

However, for such a small island, anchored 30 miles north of Kirkwall, the debate is significant. Papa Westray has for so many centuries been a backwater where money has had little or no meaning and people lived as serfs.

Now they have the opportunity to cash in and who can blame them although it might take suprisingly few extra visitors to destroy the unique spirit of peace offered by the island. This is the dilemma. Should this wild, yet homely place be preserved like some sort of northerly Inchmahome, a living museum, protected from the tramping legions of tourists, visited by appointment only or do we recognise that the community is developing, responding to change and will find its own sensible level of growth?

Learning from mistakes made elsewhere a balance must be struck between these two extremes, conservation and development.

The other element in this modern-day Orkneyinga saga is the arrival in growing numbers of incomers, white settlers, ferryloupers or just 'thae folk fae sooth?'. Compromise will be necessary in this sector too if Orkney is to benefit from an infusion of fresh blood and new ideas.

For a thousand years Orkney has accepted settlers from far afield and the happy integration of the latest batch of newcomers over the next decade is vital if the island group is to flourish. On this occasion Orkney, which has coped with Scottish annexation, Spanish castaways, Norse overlordship, not to mention the British forces during two world wars, is being asked to absorb a very diverse bunch from an outside society where values are being transformed. They comprise the disenchanted, the disaffected, those who seek solitude, beauty, those who wish to work in a society where their role is immediately discernible and not lost in the urban scramble, those who seek to be part of a strictly defined community where they can bring up their children in a safe and clean environment, a few who will patronisingly try to impose their theories of life on a sensitive and intelligent people, those who seek to be big fish in a small pond, those who cannot cope with city life and simple misfits like myself.

But blind animosity and prejudice will have to be put to one side if this union is to be achieved . . . if Orkney is not to become two societies. An understanding of the ground rules which must be applied in this coming together is essential.

New arrivals must prepare themselves psychologically for a lifestyle which is less complex, where tolerance and, above all, patience is essential. In Orkney *manyana* is often even further off than in the Latin lands. Being prepared for all eventualities (power cuts, cancelled ferries etc.) and never expecting too much are also useful disciplines. Your Sunday papers will never arrive on a Sunday and if you need a dentist then it's a flight into Kirkwall. Unwritten rules, including mucking in when required and passing the time of day with the neighbours, are common and the key for the new arrival is to follow these traditions. Start trying to change them and you might as well start looking for a new home.

But this is not one-way traffic. Islanders must exhibit understanding. Many still find it odd that people should tear themselves away from the relatively affluent South. People with influence in the community must take the lead in ensuring that if newcomers offer their talents openly, without precondition, seeking to serve rather than direct, then they must be made welcome. It must also be certain that local people, particularly young adults, are not disadvantaged in the housing or job markets.

Islanders must guard against irrational hostility prompted by strange accents and attitudes, and while it's natural for remote and sometimes embattled communities to want to weigh up new arrivals surely the incomers shouldn't have to plant three generations in the kirkyard before they're really 'at home'.

It's a humbling experience to stand on the rock shelves below St Boniface and scan the jumble of buildings and scattered masonry exposed in the bank by the summer's archaeological dig, layer upon layer of settlement from the time of Christ right through to the medieval period and beyond. These stones, a procession of pasts, which stand witness to triumph and tragedy, joy and despair, are a poignant reminder of the remarkable continuity of human endeavour on this little dot of an island.

Maybe it takes a footloose pilgrim like myself, who pays social calls on sandstone slabs and who stands just a little apart from the action, to report the important chapter currently being written in the annals of Papa Westray. Are we building Arcadia among the holms and skerries of Orkney? Is Papa Westray's golden age almost upon us? Will it even be a good try? In this land of elastic time I may not be around long enough to have these questions answered. But the stones, unmoved by transient human ambition, will note the outcome, silently. As ever.

DEREK DOUGLAS

Knitted to a Rugged Strand

The Borders of Scotland

Land of my sires! What mortal hand
Can e'er untie the filial band
That knits me to thy rugged strand.
Still, as I view each well-known scene,
Think what is now and what hath been.

SIR WALTER SCOTT, LAIRD OF ABBOTSFORD, INCURABLE ROMANTIC, sheriff of Selkirk, poet, novelist and Borderer, perfectly encapsulates in these lines from the 'Lay of the Last Minstrel' the almost umbilical draw which the Borderland exerts upon its sons and daughters.

Year upon year the exiles return from the four corners of the globe to that tract of land which we call The Borders.

They journey homewards to a landscape fashioned by almost 2,000 years of conflict. The Romans came, Hadrian built his wall but the legions were unable entirely to conquer. A massive military settlement, a garrison of occupation, was set down on the banks of the River Tweed at Melrose. They called it Trimontium from the three glorious paps of the Eildon Hills. The influence of Rome, then, was one of the earliest to make itself felt on the Borderlands.

Next came the Angles, the Vikings and the Normans. Always the narrow neck of land between the Solway and the Tyne became the cockpit of strife. By the middle of the 11th century the Scots, by force of arms, had seen off Anglo-Saxon influence in Lothian and what we now know as the Eastern Borders and the frontier between England and Scotland assumed very much the line it follows today.

There then followed almost six hundred years of bloodshed, rapine and pillage as the Wars of Independence were followed by regular outbreaks of full-scale Anglo-Scot warfare. The ruined yet still beautiful abbeys at Melrose, Kelso, Jedburgh and Dryburgh provide stark evidence of those troubled times.

These, as it were, officially sanctioned bouts of unpleasantness were interspersed with equally bloody internecine strife as the Elliots and the Douglases and the Kers and the Scotts and the Armstrongs and all the other Border families fought with each other. They quarrelled and brawled over land and cattle and matters of familial honour. These reivers of old operated what we would term today 'protection rackets' and in the process, not that they would have cared, gave the English language the word 'blackmail'.

I make no apology for dwelling on these matters martial and historical. It is simply not possible to consider and appreciate the Borders of today without at least an insight into the forces that have moulded the area and its people.

And neither, in a very real sense, in the Borderland of today is it possible to forget the past. Each year in early summer, throughout the Border towns of Hawick, Selkirk, Galashiels, Jedburgh, Langholm, and the rest, the townspeople participate in mounted pageants commemorating these bygone days.

Scott's View,
looking towards
the triple peaks of
the Eildon Hills,
Roxburghshire,
1959.

Perhaps, though, at this point, we should determine just what is meant, or at least what I consider is meant, by the term The Borders. It is not a geographically precise term and neither does it conform to any parcel of land bounded by dogmatic administrative boundaries. I suppose what I mean by The Borders would entail, in essence, the old East and Middle Marches.

Berwick, despite being in England, is on the northern bank of the Tweed and I have always considered it to be a Border town. Of Hawick, Jedburgh, Kelso, Selkirk, Galashiels, and Melrose there is no dispute. Langholm is on the eastern extremities of what I consider to be Border country but is, like the nearby village of Newcastleton, itself deep in the fierce Debateable Lands of yore, indisputably of Border pedigree.

The coastal towns and villages north of Berwick – Eyemouth, St Abbs, Cockburnspath – despite being not particularly distant from the Border line I do not consider to be Border in character. Peebles, more distant still, sneaks in while Biggar and Moffat do not. This Border-ness, then, is not a matter of milestones; it is more a matter of feel. True Borderers, and there are probably no more than 150,000 of them, know who they are even if the rest of the world does not.

But let us return to these summer cavalcades where that quality of Border-ness is celebrated each year with such vim and vigour.

In Hawick the ceremonies, taken seriously and solemnly, centre on the rout in 1514 at Hornshole on the River Teviot near the town, of a band of marauding Englishmen from Hexham. The previous year James IV and ten thousand Scots – the Flo'ers o' the Forest – had died on Flodden Field just over the Border near the village of Branxton.

Today in Hawick, as has been the case for hundreds of years, a young man, a Cornet, is chosen to be the town's standard bearer. He carries aloft the banner of blue and gold, a replica of that won from the English marauders almost five hundred years ago.

Each town's festival is accompanied by a gloriously rich store of song and verse. The basis of the Hawick celebration is splendidly portrayed in the 22 stanzas of James Hoggs' (not the Ettrick Shepherd) Common Riding song 'Teribus', the town's ancient Norse war-cry. The song dates only from 1819 but vividly depicts those dark days after Flodden, when only those too young to have died on Flodden Field were able to strike a blow against the English oppressors.

Scotia felt thine ire, O Odin!
On the bloody field of Flodden;
There our fathers fell with honour,
Round their King and country's banner

Teribus ye Teriodin,
Sons of heroes slain at Flodden,
Imitating Border bowmen,
Aye defend your rights and Common.

Hawick they left in ruins lying,
Nought was heard but widows crying;
Labour of all kinds neglected
Orphans wandering unprotected,

All were sunk in deep dejection,
None to flee to for protection;
'Till some youths who stayed from Flodden,
Rallied up by Teriodin.

Melrose Abbey.

Scott's house,
Abbotsford.

Armed with sword, with bow and quiver,
Shouting vengeance now or never!
Off they marched in martial order,
Down by Teviot's flowery border.

Down they threw their bows and arrows,
Drew their swords like veteran heroes,
Charged the foe with native valour,
Routed them and took their colour.

There are other Border festivals equally as poignant and emotive as that celebrated in Hawick, notably that of Selkirk where, again, the ceremonial centres upon the slaughter of Flodden Field and the tradition that only one man from the town survived to bring home the burgh banner and news of monstrous defeat. There is also the Festival in Jedburgh, which commemorates in part the Redeswyre Raid of 1575 when a Wardens' gathering, ironically designed as a means of settling feuds and disputes, erupted in violence. The Scottish Borderers were on the receiving end from their English counterparts until the tardy yet ultimately timeous arrival of the Jedburgh contingent bellowing their slogan 'Jethart's Here' turned rout into victory. The scene of the fray is just off the main A68 road as it crosses from Scotland into England at the Carter Bar.

I must now, though, confess to being myself a Borderer. And the choice of the Hawick Common Riding as my principal example of the Border riding festivals was not an objective one. I am from Hawick, a Teri as we call ourselves. I no longer live and work in the town, and as is the case with all exiles, absence has indeed made the heart grow fonder. Like many an exile before me it is only since quitting the green rolling hills and dales of the Borderland that I have truly come to appreciate not only the landscape but also the people and their values.

It is impossible to stay in the Borders, or to be a Borderer, without developing an appreciation for Scotland and its history. The glorious spoor of history is all around. Battles and brief encounters of a decidedly unpleasant kind have taken place all over the Border country. Ruggedly ruined peel towers with their massive stone-walls stand sentinel at valley mouths and strategic prominences.

Undoubtedly Sir Walter Scott, sent as a sickly child from Edinburgh to his grandparents' farm at Sandyknowe just a few miles south of Kelso, had his love of Scotland's history kindled in these surroundings. Nearby the farm, and now handsomely restored and open to the public, stands Smailholm Tower. From the top of the tower, where in days gone by a beacon would have been ready at all times to warn of invasion, there are clear views to the Cheviots and the Border line. Sir Walter played around the tower as a child and many a Border youngster has conjured up in his mind's eye those stirring times when Mosstroopers with lance, steel skull-cap and leather jack spurred on sweat-flecked steeds to bring home the news good and bad.

Not many, though, have been so inspired to write, as did Sir Walter, and surely with those childhood panoramas from Smailholm fresh in his poet's mind:

March, march, Ettrick and Teviotdale,
Why the deil dinna ye march forward in order?
March, march, Eskdale and Liddesdale,
All the Blue Bonnets are bound for the Border.

What a marvellously evocative incantation of the Borderlands on the march. Sir Walter and his imagination are in overdrive and we are the beneficiaries of it. But I must insert here a quibble about the literacy laird. As a Borderer one is indebted to the bard for his interest in and perpetuation of the Border ballad. Had it not been for him then scores of wonderful pieces of folklore would have been lost forever. But this same Sir Walter Scott is the man who has inflicted upon generations of Scots, and the world at large, the notion that the Highlander is the true Scot; that Highland dress, the tartan and the kilt, is the garb of the genuine Caledonian. This is, of course, nonsense and Sir Walter really should have known better. But we should not be surprised that he did not. The genius and soaring imagination of the novelist who was inspired to oversee the transformation of the splendidly named Clarty Hole by the Tweed near Galashiels to the mansion he called Abbotsford was obviously hard at work.

Entrusted with arrangements for the visit of King George IV to Edinburgh in 1822, Sir Walter contrived to swathe the capital in a madness of tartan tomfoolery. And James Stuart of Dunearn, he who had killed James Boswell's son in a dual, was moved to declare in disgust: 'Sir Walter has ridiculously made us appear a nation of Highlanders.' Quite so. But I write here as a Borderer – belligerent and cantankerous.

We tend to be like that. As a breed, Borderers are special people all the world over. They have lived their lives on the edge of uncertainty. Circumstance and environment mould a dour, resilient yet passionate race who are by costly experience and of enduring necessity suspicious of outsiders. They are hard to win over, clannish, stubborn and fiercely independent. Very probably, too, they are no respecters of high rank or position. They will judge a person on who he is, not on what he might be.

The picture, then, is not a particularly flattering one. But the attributes and outlook of the Borderer have been fashioned by the vicissitudes of the frontier.

Think of a frontier, any frontier. Are not the qualities and outlook of the folk living along its line remarkably similar? The Berliner at what used to be his wall; the settler of the old American West; the legionnaire serving at the remotest outpost of the Roman Empire; the Vietnamese villager in what used to be the demilitarized zone. Consider each of these. Do they not all display those same qualities of introspection, suspicion, and ruggedness?

Being a Borderer, then, is as much a state of mind as a matter of locality. The Scottish Borderer of today is the product of his environment, 2,000 years of survival on the front line. Is it any wonder that, for instance, the friendship of a Borderer is not something lightly given. Borderers do not deal in the easy camaraderie, the inconsequential, hail-fellow-well-met friendships of other airts where the bestowal of friendship is easy and meaningless.

The Borders of today reflects those qualities of hardy independence and insularity. Unlike in the cities, rugby football is the game of the people, that of the working man. There really is no other game which would have been so suited to the Border character, and Scotland as a whole is in debt to the Border clubs for their contribution to the national cause.

The staple industries of the Borders are still hosiery, tweed and farming but the area was, too, one of the first to be sampled by the incoming electronics industry.

Borderers do have a fine regard for heritage and the traditions of the past. Occasionally such regard for what has 'aye been' can look foolish as in Hawick's insistence that the town's first lady provost cannot participate in some of the Common Riding ceremonial. But such homage to history

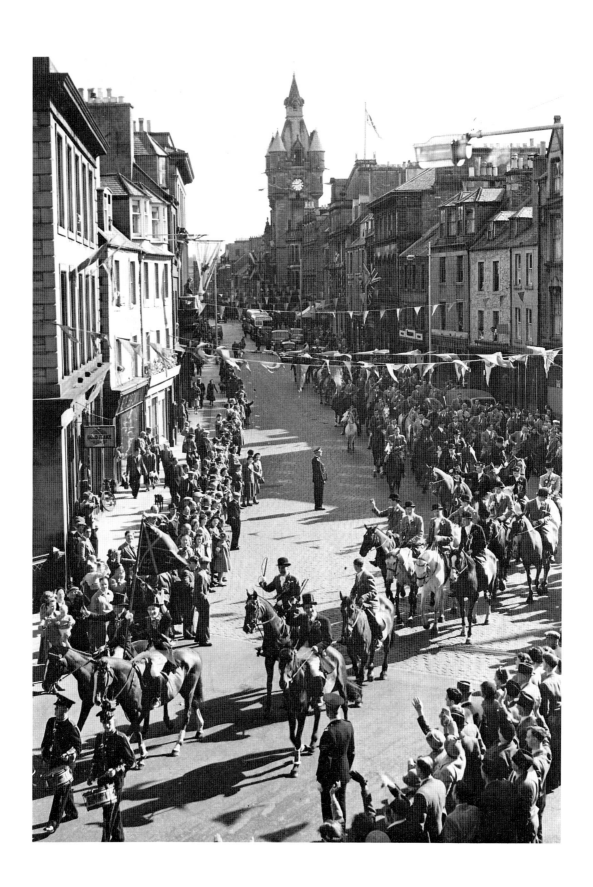

Through the streets
of Coldstream to
Flodden, 1952.

as exists never has, and never will, degenerate to the levels of malignancy of, for instance, Ulster where blind devotion to the past has left its present inhabitants with a bleak future indeed.

But let us end with another song. William Sanderson's 'Sweet Lowland Tongue o' The Borders' perfectly encaptures the feelings which the Borderland kindles in its sons and daughters. The opening verse and chorus will suffice and the sentiments expressed therein will strike a chord with exiled Borderers wherever they may be.

> O blithe is the lilt o' his ain mither tongue,
> To the exile that's long been a-roamin'.
> It brings back tae mind the auld songs that were sung
> Roon his faither's fireside at the gloamin'.
> It brings back the scent o' the heathery braes,
> The soond o' the wee burnie's wimple,
> The laughin', the daffin' o' youth's happy days,
> When his cheeks' deepest line was a dimple.
> What though in the ha's o' the great we may meet,
> Wi' men o' high rank and braw orders,
> Oor hearts sigh for hame
> And nae music sae sweet
> As the soft lowland tongue o' the Borders.

Smailholm Tower.

DOUGLAS DUNN

A City Discovered

Dundee

THE PANORAMA FROM DUNDEE LAW IS ONE OF ASTOUNDING DISTANCES
and beauty. For a few moments, local and Scottish time and space are held
in an exhilarating but probably illusory perspective in which past and present
seem to coexist in a single tense. While the war memorial (Hugh MacDiarmid
thought it looked mean) reminds you of the worst of the 20th century, that
broad, visual experience of the Firth of Tay, with its blue Scottish hazes, its
river-colours, its greens, yellows, golds, greys and silvers, brings you back to
thoughts of the best of life.

To the west you look towards Perth over the Carse of 'many-birded
Gowrie'. Turning a little you can see the Grampian core and its footnotes, the
Sidlaws. Over all that land west, north and east, the hand of man has moved
with benign, agricultural influence. Place names like Barns of Wedderburn
and Barns of Claverhouse pin two famous local families to the map. Of the
first, one was Bishop of St Andrews in the 16th century and wrote most of
The Gude and Godlie Ballatis. 'Bonnie Dundee' was the celebrated Graham
of Claverhouse:

> But the Provost, douce man, said: Just e'een let him be,
> The guid toun is weel quit of that dell o' Dundee.

From Broughty Castle north along the Angus coast you can make out clearly
beaches, links, Buddon's military ranges and as far past Carnoustie as the
state of your eyesight will permit. Daniel Defoe evoked Angus as 'bespangled
and fruitful'. It still is. He found its people angry at the Union. Some of them
still are.

In the south lies the whole of north Fife with Newburgh, Balmerino,
Wormit, Newport and Tayport on the south bank of the Tay. You can
see the bulk of the Lomonds behind them in the distance, beyond the
invisible bottomlands of the Howe of Fife. Your eye crosses Fife's eastern
peninsula to Tentsmuir, the Eden estuary and St Andrews Bay. Where
the Tay meets the sea there might be a deceptively-static white line to
indicate the force with which the ocean encounters the power of the
river – the Tay empties more water into the sea than any other river
in the archipelago. There might be moments of high dazzle on the water
anywhere from east to west and back again. Swift cloud-shadows can drop
sudden darkenings and brightenings on both water and land, neither of which
stays unchanged for long. The Tay Road Bridge is practically below you. It
runs in a dramatic, technological straight line. From up here the rail bridge
looks fragile. Tricks of light can make it shift and shiver. There could be
a coaster heading for the port of Perth. East of the road bridge you might
see oil-rig tenders, freighters, coasters, and, sometimes, sleek, grey bearers of
NATO deathware. Especially in summer, the Tay can be dotted with yachts
and dinghies. It is a big prospect, all 360 degrees of it. Dundee Law, however,
is an urban outlook tower as well. It sets the whole of Dundee in its land- and
waterscapes.

Discovery, *Dundee*,
1990.

•

Dundee is a neglected city. Relatively few Scots seem to know much about it, but, like anywhere else in Scotland, you could go round its map noting its lore, some of it trivial, some of it momentous, until the pen fell from your hand. Dundee is not a secret to its citizens, but until recently they were happy to endure, perhaps even to enjoy, being out on the limb of an indifferent reputation. They were content to be identified by the cipher of 'jute, jam and journalism', or as the place where the bridge fell into the river, or the city where a teetotal, ban-the-drink candidate ousted Winston Churchill from his seat, or as the town with two football teams, one on either side of the road. Some visitors expect to see small boys in dungarees carrying buckets while giving the slip to Boab-like constables. Others have been known to report that the population looks suspiciously like an extended family of Broons. But it would be unwise, offensive and inaccurate to describe individual Dundonians as stereotypes of the city's populist journalism, or as complacent, or to suggest that the city as a whole is politically timid, careless of identity or lacking in one. In the *Dundee Courier* and the *Sunday Post* they have the most Conservative and faithfully subscribed newspapers in Scotland, but they vote as if they have never heard of their editorial lines. It speaks for a certain presence of mind. The character of Dundee is like that of anywhere else in Scotland, only more so. A friend tells me – but don't ask me how he knows – that more porridge is eaten in Dundee, Angus and Fife than anywhere else in the country. He believes that this mysterious statistic explains just about everything.

Like most of Scotland, until a few years ago Dundee gave every impression of being exhausted. It was worn out by its industries. Through the 19th century its population and industrial capacity grew fast and steadily. By 1841 its population stood at 65,000, an increase by a third over the previous decade and explained by a thriving linen industry. Emigration from rural Scotland and Ireland was encouraged to feed the constant and growing demand for cheap labour, with, as a result, the creation of urban squalor at least the equal of Glasgow's. By 1850 Dundee was being described as 'Juteopolis'. It was to carry out practically all the preparation of jute undertaken in Britain. Linen and canvas continued to be important: Dundee was a major centre of sail-making. Ancillary trades and industries were developed to support the jute mills. For centuries it had been a busy port, dealing especially in the timber, flax and hides of the Baltic trade, although, earlier, it had been a significant importer of wine. Shipbuilding and other maritime interests grew as the jute industry accelerated. By 1911 its population had climbed to 165,000, not far off the figure of 179,674 established by the 1981 Census, although, according to an estimate made in June 1988, it has fallen to 174,255.

One industry often gives rise to the ingenuity that creates another. In 1832 a Dundonian discovered that jute could be treated with whale oil and made workable by machine. Dundee's whalers guaranteed the oil. British India guaranteed regular harvests and shipments of jute, a vegetable fibre gathered from the bark of the plants *Corchorus capsularia* and *C. olitorius*. The English word 'jute' comes from Bengali via Sanskrit, and the last step of its etymology means 'a braid of hair'; it is an affecting, and, perhaps, feminine irony when you bear in mind that a large proportion of the jute industry's workforce were women. Fortunes were made from jute, and from the labour that harvested it, shipped it, and that worked it into sacking, bagging, canvas and gunny. It was Victorian plastic. Commerce's appetite for cheap sacking and bagging devoured Dundee's production, which wars stimulated. Military commissariats consumed tons of the stuff – sacks for their supplies, nosebags,

Sunrise at Cox's Stack, Dundee, 1980.

Sunset on the River Tay looking towards Dundee, 1960.

sandbags for the construction of embrasures, whether in the Crimean War, both sides in the American Civil War, conflicts in Europe, or for the needs of the British imperial forces. By the time of the First World War profiteering was blatant enough for the government to intervene and control the prices of jute products during a war that went through more sandbags than anyone knows. Even by then, though, stiff competition from Dundee-controlled and other Indian factories had encouraged the jute kings to diversify, chiefly into finance, the art of using wealth to make even more.

Lord Cockburn wrote of Edinburgh that nothing that stuck up there without smoking ever looked ill. Apart from church steeples everything that stuck up in Dundee smoked like the enormous industrial lums that they were. Cox's Stack in Lochee (around 15,000 were employed in Lochee's mills at one time) was by far the most massive of these chimneys. It stood 280 feet high and was erected in the mid-1860s, presumably on profits from the American Civil War. It was built of red and white brick in the form of an Italianated campanile. Now whittled down by fire and demolition, it remains an impressive stump. Its height alleviated at least some of the smoke pollution that issued from Camperdown and other mills and enshrouded whole districts. That it was built at all suggests a degree of concern for the well-being of the jute workers and their families. As elsewhere in Scotland, Victorian industrial avarice had its obverse in philanthropy, in libraries, swimming baths and football pitches. There was little that could be done about the mills themselves. They were noisy, foul-smelling, and exhausting places.

In 1921 four times as many married women worked full-time in Dundee than in Glasgow. Cheap female labour was used as a means of competing with the even cheaper costs of jute factories on the Hooghly River. More than likely it passed through the minds of Dundonian proprietors that Indian factories were canny hedges against the consequences of union-organised labour and bigger wage bills at home. It was a competitive strategy that did more than risk the ruination of their countrymen; it courted it. Before 1914 large numbers of children, mainly girls – they came just that bit cheaper – were employed in the jute mills. Some worked a 12-hour day at a time when Indian law limited daily juvenile employment to seven hours. To working people child and female labour were part of a way of life that was slow to change. Quite possibly the Dundee School Board believed that exemptions from attendance were acts of kindness. Low adult wages kept many families on the breadline. Sickness, incapacity, imprisonment, or the death of a parent, were all it took to turn poverty into wretchedness. A child's daily coppers could have made all the difference in the days when women worked 'Tae feed an' cled ma bairnie affen ten an' nine'.

Small wonder, then, that Dundee produced a brutalised working class, and a brutalising, douce aristocracy of employers who could withdraw behind the trappings of elegance on the leafy, manorial slopes of Broughty Ferry or wherever. Not for nothing was it known as 'the city of dreadful Knights'. George Blake called it 'an East Coast city with a West Coast temperament' which sounds neat, but is doubtfully true. What he might have meant is that Dundee, like Glasgow, shared in common a large minority of Irish origin and a slender middle class. Blake was writing about Scotland as a whole, and, as even gifted Scots are prone to do, he strained for 'differences' where mutual predicaments might have come closer to the truth. Were the more parochial commentators believed, Scotland differs *strikingly* parish by parish, never mind in a comparison between its cities and regions. Variousness, if understood more deeply, might be a unifying phenomenon rather than

West Port, Dundee,
1981.

one that splits a citizenshipless nationality into imaginary provinces. Now that characteristic industries have dwindled or gone, what Dundee can be seen to share with Glasgow (and with much of Scotland as a whole) is a real working-class profile that is vulnerable to exaggeration and caricature. It leads to prideful wallows in the industrial and social past and to a retrogressive state of mind that postpones prosperity and furtherance. It can sometimes seem that working-class Scots are scared stiff of the benefits of education and modernity in case they transform them into members of the hated bourgeoisie.

'Dundee, the palace of Scottish blackguardism, unless perhaps Paisley be entitled to contest this honour with it,' Lord Cockburn wrote in 1844. He lost no time in making for St Andrews, there to meditate among the ruins. His rapid transition from Dundonian criminality to the fragrant antiquities of St Andrews is another syndrome that we could do without. 'Dundee, a sink of atrocity, which no moral flushing seems capable of cleansing', he wrote eight years later when Juteopolis had become a reality:

> A Dundee criminal, especially if a lady, may be known, without any evidence about character, by the intensity of the crime, the audacious bar air, and the parting curses. What a set of she-devils were before us! Mercy on us! if a tithe of the subterranean execration that they launched against us, after being sentenced, was to be as effective as they wished it, commination never was more cordial.

Cocky judged and wrote before much credence was given to the causes of crime other than a vague predisposition to theft, murder or mayhem; but his 'witty,' dismissive generalisations are typical of the carelessness with which Dundee was and continues to be assessed. His old-fashioned rural sympathies left him incapable of understanding Dundee as a boom town which, from the point of view of working people, could support life, while to entrepreneurs it offered the opulence of Victorian civilisation. It was on the industrial frontier, a Klondike to which emigrants made their way in search of life's pittance. In some districts it was livelihood's roughhouse, a cross between a sweatshop and Hell's Kitchen. It becomes understandable that Dundee should have produced an expert in Christian self-denial like Mary Slessor who began life as a child mill-worker. Some aspects of her character make her seem as formidable as those Dundonian viragos that Cockburn sentenced to imprisonment, transportation or the gallows. 'She was capable of wresting from a man a rifle which she considered he should not have,' one writer has reported, 'and even the corrosive epithet was not beyond her'. Or, as Mary Kingsley wrote of 'the Queen of Okoyong', 'the sort of man Mary Slessor represents is rare'. William Lyon Mackenzie, although an earlier, pre-jute figure, also becomes understandable. He issued from the radical Dundee of the late 1810s, the ornament of which was George Kinloch, 'the radical laird'. Before that there was the English parson Thomas Palmer, transported to Australia with Muir of Huntershill, and whose crime was the publication of an address from the Dundee Friends of Liberty. Mackenzie trained himself to be a first-rate pain in the neck of the Canadian colonial government. It is easy to imagine where his resentments began.

Like Mary Slessor he would have harried his opponents in what the late Wilfred taylor described as 'probably the most ugly accent in Scotland', but 'intensely virile'.

> Dundonians talk as though they would never allow themselves to be imposed on by anyone, and the thick, gutteral sounds they produce are rich in sceptical

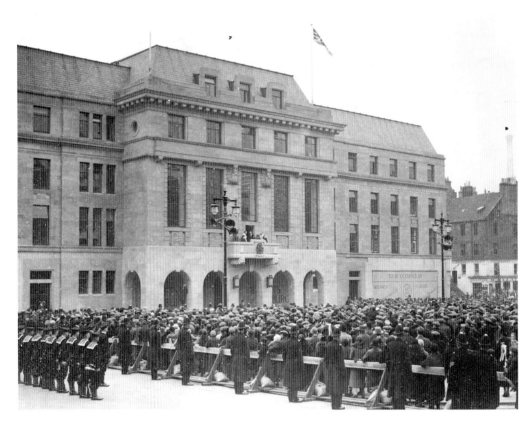

Prince George opens the new City Chambers, Dundee, 1933.

A Tay sail on the Scotscraig, better known to Dundonians as the 'Fyfey', Dundee, 1954.

undertones. I cannot recall, as a Dundonian myself, ever having heard a Dundee mother singing a lullaby to her babe, but I imagine that the general effect would be to provoke the average babe into a state of uncompromising belligerency. Dundee . . . is the chief breeding ground of the glottal stop. More artistry is put into glottal stoppage in Dundee than in any other part of the world.

Patrick Geddes was professor of botany at the university and his biographer evoked the city as 'Scotland's ugliest town', a sprawl of 'prison-like grey factories' and 'prison-like grey slums' placed 'in the most beautiful natural setting imaginable'. To Lewis Grassic Gibbon Dundee in the early 1930s was 'a frowsy fisher-wife addicted to gin and infanticide'. Considering the discomforts and social problems associated with post-war and even more recent housing stock, Scottish cities would seem burdened with eternal sorrow. As early as 1915, in his book *Cities in Evolution*, Patrick Geddes was dismayed by the mentality that invites squalor:

> . . . when, as of course now and then of late years, some little Housing discussion is raised in Scotland, the tenements, and even their one- and two-roomed components, still find no lack of advocates, and these among all classes! Not only do individuals speak in their defence, but even local pride is aroused. The fact is, we rather look down upon small brick houses: we admire our lofty piles of stone: we still use their historic and legal name of 'Lands'. Finally, the whole matter is put upon what are really high metaphysical grounds (which 'the practical man' is ever so liable to wander into). We are made to feel a certain fitness in these things, a certain established harmony; in fact a sort of foreordination of Scotsmen for tenements and tenements for Scotsmen. Upon these towering heights of national destiny, therefore, the economic verdict is easy to give, and hard to refuse – that 'we can afford nothing better'. Economic explanations are added by some, and political explanations of these by others: none of them sufficient. But without this abstract and philosophical turn, in fact this theological dignity of argument, the proposition – that the printers and masons of Edinburgh, the shipbuilders and engineers of Glasgow, all admittedly second to none in their production, are to be in their economic consumption second to all, and that permanently – would be realized in all its flagrant absurdity.

As in other Scottish cities, Dundee's housing problems (and they were stark) were tackled with ill-conceived schemes and estates. Tenemented 'lofty piles' and clapped out factories were pulled down and replaced by loftier structures on the same sites. At least temporarily, or in principle, it was undertaken with municipal decency, but tainted with that 'second to all' mentality that Patrick Geddes exposed all of 75 years ago. Dundee hardly deserves to be singled out for having failed to break the intellectual, political and financial barriers that cramped, and that continue to hinder, local authorities in Scotland. To a large extent it is victimised by the exceptional promise of its position. Preliminary cries of delight often turn out to be prologues to critical hysteria. Whether approaching by road or rail, by either bridge from the south, disappointment seems to overtake visitors unprepared to understand why Dundee is as it is. It grew too quickly from its ancient mercantile centre. Gradual, organic development, in touch with sympathetic local architectural talent, was never on the cards, with, as a result, the state of mind that defied national opinion in the early 1930s when William Adam's Town House of 1732 was demolished. Whatever their gifts for domestic ostentation, or, later, municipal window-dressing, jute's nabobs and others in a position to influence Dundee's appearance possessed neither the time, the inclination or the civilising intellectual goodwill equal to the requirements of

Mary Slessor, 1848-1915.

benign city-making. Misled by the Tay's breadth, the panoramic splendour of its basin, visitors expect a different city, one that expresses the geography, not the history of the place. Having said that, it has to be pointed out that Dundee's city centre has its moments. There are enough of them to remind you of what is easily forgotten, that to a large extent we live in 19th-century cities which recent times have eroded rather than transformed. As a result, newer developments in Dundee like the Overgate shopping centre and the Wellgate Centre can feel uncomfortably modern as well as immune to the dignity of ageing. They look like commercial expedients.

Nor are developments on the riverside west of the road bridge calculated to inspire. The Earl Grey Hotel might even be the worst new building in Scotland. While the swimming pool and leisure centre are splendid and necessary amenities, if they had to be built there then a more imaginative or even playful structure might have been more appropriate. At the Dundee end of the road bridge, just to the left of the toll gate, Dundonian humour has contrived to hang plastic lemons on the high branches of trees. Motorists have been subject to double-takes. Perhaps what it is trying to say is that Dundee, too, might be an illusion. It is a good-natured prank, and worth being grateful for; a moment later, when you see Tayside Regional Council's Tayside House, a blank austerity of a building that, without meaning to, states a government's low opinion of itself and the governed, you can laugh at it.

Someone once said that given Dundee's natural site what it needs is the equivalent of the Sydney Opera House. It would seem to me to be neither what the site nor Dundonians could abide. There is something detectable in the pride of Dundonians that makes you feel that they dislike drawing attention to themselves. An absence of self-assertion need not be vicious or cowardly in individuals or a community. It could be that working-class profile again, but it is more likely to be a native distrust of the showy. Dundee suffered bigger blows to its economy than any other city in Scotland. Its people have been down, but they have got up again. It is not a glamorous city or a wealthy one; its history has seen to that, although the signs are that it is close to having shaken itself free of a pitiless industrial past. Nor is it insensitive to the arts. The SNO performs in the Caird Hall, Dundee Repertory Theatre presents imaginative seasons and is handsomely housed, there is a good Central Library in the Wellgate Centre, and municipal galleries and museums. The university, Duncan of Jordanstone College of Art and other colleges, of commerce and technology, stimulate the arts and in some fields are right up there with the best of them anywhere else.

Scotland is supposed to dote on education, yet its benefits look to be percolating through to the general environment with painful lethargy. 'Think of Florence, Paris, London, New York,' says Alasdair Gray's character Thaw in *Lanark*:

> Nobody visiting them for the first time is a stranger because he's already visited them in paintings, novels, history books and films. But if a city hasn't been used by an artist not even the inhabitants live there imaginatively.

Dundee has produced relatively few writers. In the 19th century the minister George Gilfillan was a critic to be reckoned with, and his essays were felt interesting enough to be reprinted in Everyman's Library in 1909. It is disturbing, but true – William MacGonagall's eccentric celebrity is taken as identifying the town's artistic spirit, he who, as Hugh MacDiarmid put it, was not a bad poet, he was not a poet of any kind. Dundee shares with the

*Discovering
recovery, Dundee,
1990.*

Remembering what is gone, Dundee, 1990.

*Tea-time at
McManus Art
Gallery, Dundee,
1990.*

John Byrne,
Dundee, 1988.

other cities of modern Scotland, with the exception of Edinburgh, the state of having been under-imagined and over-criticised. Both Lewis Spence and Sir Alexander Gray were natives of Dundee but neither, so far as I know, wrote about the city. It probably participated in Grassic Gibbon's 'Duncairn' in *Grey Granite*, along with Aberdeen. 'Dundee is dust', Hugh MacDiarmid wrote in one of his poems; and that was that. Much of Scotland was simply rejected by its writers and artists. While it testifies to the affront of industrial horror, poverty and careless government, it indicates, too, that something was lacking in artistic determination earlier in this century, particularly in literature. If nothing else, though, it leaves writers with a clear sense of the ground that has to be made up. It might also suggest to them that identification with a district can be of artistic assistance, to the writers and to the place. Plays of local interest have appeared at the Dundee Rep and proved successful. Several writers live in the Dundee district – notably the playwright John Byrne, the social historian and playwright Billy Kay, the playwright Gordon Burnside, and several younger poets, including John Glenday. Otherwise the success of the art college tends to identify the area by painters including the doyen of Scottish landscape painting James McIntosh Patrick, Alberto Morrocco, and Will Malean. There are many more.

In calling itself the 'City of Discovery', after Captain Scott's ship, which was built in Dundee, the city does more than angle its publicity through a relic of the past in celebration of defunct whaling and the shipbuilding that went with it. It appeals to itself as well as to the rest of the world. It asks its own people to discover where they live and what they can do to improve themselves and their place. Dundee is recommending itself, as well it should, but its character is such that rude touting would stick in its craw. There is a decent, unpretentious momentum to the new temperament of Dundee. What other city in Scotland could have chosen a concept like 'discovery' with its inevitable two-way implications? Officially, it is eight hundred years old. It has come a long way since it stuck its neck out for Sir William Wallace, and a long way since Daniel Defoe depicted Dundee as a city of gentleman merchants. As a district in which to live, it is addictive. The landscapes of its hinterlands in Angus and Forfar (and Fife, although Fifers often object to the association) remind me of Hugh MacDiarmid's amusedly indignant line: 'Scotland small? Our multiform, our infinite Scotland *small*?' But for the most part it is a matter of the 'passionate' Tay. Lewis Spence could get away from it no more than I can:

> As haars the windless waters find
> The unguarded instant falls a prey
> To sakeless shadows o' the mind,
> And a' my life rins back to Tay.
>
> Deep in the saul the early scene –
> Ah, let him play wi' suns wha can,
> The cradle's pented on the een,
> The native airt resolves the man!

GRAEME SMITH

The Northern Lights

Aberdeen

THE GRANITE CITY IS LOSING ITS SPARKLE – IT IS BEING TARNISHED BY progress.

The discovery of oil in the North Sea has given Aberdeen almost all it could want – wealth, employment, entertainment, the chance of security for future generations – but the city is letting its greatest assets slide through its fingers.

Its character, its couthiness, the pride its citizens have always felt because their city was different is slipping away.

The unflappable Aberdonians have grasped the opportunities which oil presented, and although they are leaders in a high tech world, they have retained their characteristics, which have been immortalised by comedians like *Scotland the What?*

The same cannot be said about their city.

Its main artery, Union Street, will never be as empty as the postcards show when 'mean' Aberdonians stay indoors on a flag day but life is ebbing away from it into new faceless shopping arcades. Many of the solid granite buildings designed by Archbishop Simpson and John Smith which make Union Street one of the most attractive in Britain have been left empty, ugly and abandoned by chain stores who prefer to be housed in bright, shiny, air-conditioned malls which add nothing to the city's image.

Woolworths opened up in Union Street in 1926 but they have moved indoors. C&A's has gone to the same giant complex, although people still meet at C&A's corner, its home for decades. Their business sense has led them to the Bon Accord Centre, a £60 million complex which is not only drawing the life from Union Street but has severed its link with Aberdeen's second street, George Street. Not so long ago buses turned off Union Street and continued up George Street but now even the pedestrian route is through the heavy doors of the St Nicholas Centre and then the doors of the Bon Accord Centre, all locked at night.

The heart of the city has been transplanted, ironically to the area where Aberdeen's first mall was built. In 1905 'The Co-opie' – the Northern Co-operative Society – built an arcade which was ahead of its time but, alas, was not preserved. The granite-fronted mall with its high glass roof and tiled walls in which housewives queued to collect their 'divi', then queued to spend it, was demolished.

Many of the new stores have been lured north by the fact that while Aberdeen houses only four per cent of Scotland's population it has double that percentage of the country's spending power. That undoubtedly is due to the discovery of oil in the North Sea and oil is still the key to Aberdeen's future and to restoration of its sparkle.

The next few years are crucial. Aberdeen is Europe's oil capital but to become a force to be reckoned with worldwide, and not just a North Sea service centre, it will have to show the vision and determination it displayed when it saw the riches oil could bring. Success will safeguard the cosy lifestyle to which we have become accustomed.

The passenger ship
St Helena *acquires*
its funnel, Aberdeen,
1990.

*Union Street, near
Holburn Junction,
Aberdeen, 1955.*

With the economy buoyant and interest in Aberdeen intense we must cash in. We must win the battle for improved rail and air links to the city which has been the focal point for the industry which has helped keep Britain solvent for the last 15 years. We have finally succeeded in gaining a tolerable road to the South, at least by Scottish standards, but the road to the North is a dangerous disgrace.

Tourism will be vital to Aberdeen in the 21st century and to force us on to the competitive international scene the money men must be persuaded to invest the £20 million required to fulfil the city's dream of 'The Oil Experience Centre' – a flagship Disney World-type complex on the promenade. It will take that kind of imaginative project to bring the tourists back to the golden sands which were once alive with holidaymakers before package tours sent them flocking to the Mediterranean.

However, it is typical of Aberdeen that as the talking went on about the grandiose plan to create this tourist attraction, the original buildings which generations remember as the centrepoint of the beach were allowed to deteriorate to such an extent they were demolished.

It is only fair to say that there are numerous outstanding examples of conservation within the city, but unfortunately the worst neglect is where it matters most.

Another example is just a stone's throw from the Bon Accord Centre with its glass and chrome and the St Nicholas Centre with its doors which frail old ladies find impossible to open. A century and a half ago Archibald Simpson designed the Triple Kirks whose graceful brick spire is a city-centre landmark. A smart restaurant occupies one refurbished church-building but for more than a decade the future of the remainder has been undecided and vandalism and the harsh North-East weather have taken their toll. Safety concerns have forced the demolition of parts of the irreplaceable building and there are fears that unless something is done with a haste which is alien to Aberdonians their treasured spire will disappear from the landscape.

The lack of urgency which has allowed the Triple Kirks to crumble must be avoided in the revitalisation of Union Street.

Granted, the District Council were swift to implement discussions when the Union Street decline reached crisis point, but that was far too late and they are speaking about restoring it to its former glory in time for its 200th birthday – at the turn of the century.

A lack of urgency is not an unusual trait in Aberdonians and has contributed to the charm of the city – its pace is slower than most. But it is time the zest displayed when the North Sea's riches were uncovered was on show again.

Aberdeen's economy was in decline when oil was discovered in BP's Forties Field in 1970, creating a massive opportunity for the city which had always depended heavily on other natural resources. The post-war industries of fishing, food processing, paper-making, textiles and shipbuilding were in decline and Aberdeen increasingly was reliant on its position as the main service centre for the North-East and the Northern Isles.

Spurred by competition for the title of Europe's oil capital from other East Coast British ports and Scandinavia and Germany, the Aberdonians, never known to rush into anything, burst into action and left the others in their wake. Land was made available for housing and industrial developments, the harbour board invested millions to support the offshore activity, Aberdeen Airport was transformed from a series of huts and a heliport was created which became the world's busiest.

Aberdeen turned truly cosmopolitan with American, French and Dutch

The Netherkirkgate, Aberdeen, 1933.

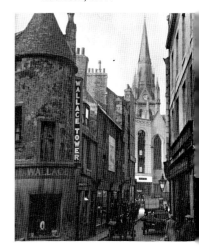

*Aberdeen City
Police Pipe Band
at Union Terrace
Gardens, Aberdeen,
1959.*

*Draughts at Union
Terrace Gardens,
Aberdeen, 1959.*

schools among the 40 new ones which opened. In Union Street, where there were not enough shops to spend the oil dollars, a Texas drawl was as common as a 'fit' or a 'foo'. House prices rocketed and there was an air of cockiness about the city. It would have been more convenient for the government, commerce and industry if the oil capital of Europe had been situated in the more accessible Central Belt or even England, but they had no choice. Good fortune and swift action had combined to give Aberdeen its chance.

It mattered little then, and for more than a decade, that the traditional industries were declining. The oil companies were desperate to get the oil ashore and were prepared to throw money at problems. Earnings swept from 15 per cent below the national average to more than the same above. Prestige office developments sprung up around the city. Oil majors built their headquarters on Hill of Rubislaw, perched on the edge of Europe's largest man-made hole – the disused and water-filled quarry from which the granite which gave the city its nickname was hewn.

We Aberdonians were smug. We always knew we had as much going for us as Glasgow or Edinburgh and that Dundee didn't merit a second thought, except perhaps just before the oil era when our fortunes slid, the population declined, and Dundee posed a genuine threat of becoming Scotland's third city. But we beat them to the oil riches and were enjoying being a city of prosperity. Not only were there fashionable restaurants attracted by the big expense accounts but prestigious shops were opening up and for me, returning to Aberdeen within weeks of the Queen pressing the button which started the oil flowing ashore in 1975, one of the most noticeable features was a marked lack of cars more than two or three years old.

Aberdonians had been quick to adapt to their new lifestyle. The ladies who had been consistently behind in fashion demanded designer wear to keep up with the white settlers moving in. Businessmen who had previously regarded a drive to Dundee as a long journey were up and down to London by air from a new international airport. Ordinary Aberdonians were as likely to get a Sikorsky S61 helicopter to work as a 23 bus, and, true to form, were completely unphased by it all. In time yuppie wine-bars opened for young oilmen and entrepreneurs with their Filofaxes, their cabriolets and their gold cards with which they paid for their expensive meals.

The city was sparkling.

Men who would have become joiners or electricians in another city became roughnecks, roustabouts, divers or derrickmen in Aberdeen. Wives and children had to adjust to absent husbands and fathers for two weeks at a time. The traditional industries suffered as their workforces took to the helicopters and headed out to oilfields like Beryl and Brent whose names became as familiar as Torry and Cults.

The oil industry drew people from all over the world to Aberdeen. Many came reluctantly but departed even more reluctantly when the time came to move on. Aberdeen gave them a floral welcome whether they arrived from the north, south or west. Then, as now, in spring the greeting was in daffodils and crocuses, in summer a million roses.

It is an unrivalled floral city. Its proud boast is that it won the Britain in Bloom award so many times it was banned to give others a chance. It is dotted with parks, large and small, with features like a blind garden where visitors can appreciate the flowers by their scent. The Duthie Park's Winter Gardens are allegedly one of Britain's top tourist attractions although I suspect that the machine at the door which keeps count is unable to spot the habitual visitors there to read their Sunday paper or simply in for a 'heat-up'.

Aberdeen, 1990.

Aberdeen Harbour, 1948.

Discussing the catch after the fish auctions at Aberdeen Harbour, 1990.

Aberdeen old and new, 1990.

*The Bon Accord
Centre with its
distinctive dome,
Aberdeen, 1990.*

Side-street shop,
Aberdeen, 1990.

Scotland the What? would probably claim that the locals at the tropical paradise were only there to save coal. They perpetuate the myth, if it is a myth, that Aberdonians are mean. Although their talents are now appreciated abroad – in places like Edinburgh and London – they are best loved in their home city because Aberdonians love to laugh at themselves, especially the dignitaries who can only say they've made it when they are the subject of the team's humour.

One of their early sketches involves an Aberdonian making a speech at his daughter's wedding and explaining that because of the cost of the meal everyone could not be invited. That was why his wife was at the bingo!

The Laird of Inversnecky, the great Harry Gordon, would have you believe that Aberdonians took corners on two wheels to save wear on their tyres. But whether we are mean or not – and apparently no one gives more to charity than the folk from the North-East – we can offer a priceless attraction in our city. Quality of life. We have documentary evidence from the University of Glasgow to show that the education standards are second to none and that in terms of health care, shopping facilities and sports facilities we are amongst the best in Britain.

This was appreciated by the oil incomers many of whom had long-term plans for life in the Granite City, plans which suddenly changed in 1986. Unfortunately what goes up must come down and in that year the oil price plummeted from $30 to $10 in less than a month, rocking Aberdeen on its heels. Just as no one had foreseen the impact on Aberdeen of the advent of the oil no one had anticipated the effect the drop would have.

Oil jobs vanished, drilling rigs lay idle off the East Coast and in Aberdeen the effect was devastating. The city had been bucking national trends. It had been on the crest of a wave when the rest of the country was in the doldrums and the downturn was harder to swallow because elsewhere the economy was buoyant.

Just as quickly as the house prices had climbed they sank, sometimes with grave financial consequences. Those who had bought just before the

*Pilot Square,
Aberdeen, 1990.*

crash and had to move on because they had lost their jobs sacrificed small fortunes. Many Americans forced to return to their homeland found it impossible to sell and posted their keys to the building societies, who had loaned them their mortgages, challenging them to find a buyer. Some tried auctioning their homes. Others offered inducements like a free car. In one street alone, albeit a long one, I counted 35 houses for sale in February 1986.

Even the football team hit a slump. In 1983 Alex Ferguson had guided them to their greatest triumph when they lifted the European Cup Winners Cup in Gothenburg, but Manchester United lured him away in 1986 and the Dons fortunes followed those of the oil industry.

Aberdeen went from boom to gloom and the city suddenly realised how dependant it had become on the oil industry. Plans for the future were drawn up, plans to give Aberdeen a broader-based economy, plans which were launched with an enthusiasm which seems to have waned now that the oil industry is again on the crest of a wave.

I fear that although we Aberdonians have learned some lessons in the last few years, we have slipped back into our smug complacency.

House prices have soared again, skills shortages are pushing the oil salaries up, the harbour is bustling, and the dons are back amongst the silverware. The loss of 167 lives in the Piper Alpha disaster, just as the industry was dusting itself down after the slump, left a permanent scar on the city but was never allowed to slow down the resurgence.

The oil will not provide us with riches for ever but there are bright prospects ahead well into the 1990s, giving Aberdeen another chance to carve a secure future. In 1986 as the oil jobs evaporated at the rate of 1,000 a month it seemed that the cars were not as new and shiny as they had been and, on the rear windows of many, stickers begged: 'Please God, Give Us a Second Oil Boom', promising in less than reverend terms not to waste another chance.

The second oil boom has arrived but whether the promise will be fulfilled remains to be seen.

ALF YOUNG

Movers and Shakers

Scotland's Young Entrepreneurs

WRITE ABOUT SCOTLAND'S YOUNG ENTREPRENEURS, THEY TOLD ME. THAT won't take up much space, snorted one amused cynic, clearly convinced that, when it comes to boardroom movers and shakers on the youthful side of 40, say, Scotland's contribution to the talent pool ranks somewhere between our standing in world cricket and our reputation for winemaking.

That cynicism is shared by some of the business builders themselves. I recall, in the spring of 1985, going to interview the then relatively unknown David Murray, the previous year's recipient of the Scottish Business Achievement Award. Murray was scathing about the 'four hour lunchers' whose business achievement was best measured by their ever-expanding girth.

'There are too many people in business in this country who spend all their time talking about it,' he broadsided. 'Too many maybes, would-haves and could-dos.' In the years since, as Murray's own business empire has expanded, adding electronic sub-assembly, property development and control of Rangers Football Club to the core steel-stockholding companies, I have heard him return many times to that same theme.

'Where is the next generation of David Murrays?' he will demand, lambasting the stranglehold of the professions, the shortcomings of the educational system, the Scot's propensity to pull down anyone who tries to climb too far out of their own midden, or some other perceived weakness in the way we embrace enterprise.

The facts tend to support Murray's fears. Regional VAT returns demonstrate that we create proportionately fewer new businesses than other parts of the UK. Our managers chase fewer buy-outs. Too many of those who do succeed in building viable businesses sell on their creation before it has realised its full potential. Few Scottish growth companies achieve a Stock Market listing, and too many of those which do find the experience painful or, in some cases, terminal.

The picture used to look very different. Scotland had more than its share of 18th and 19th century entrepreneurs, grasping every opportunity the newly industrialised age offered. So what's happened to their late 20th-century descendants? To the party of enterprise, currently occupying St Andrew's House, today's Scots are too hooked on what others will do for us, products of a dependency culture whose roots run stubbornly deep.

There may be a grain of truth in that simplistic analysis, although I'm not sure I'm prepared to buy it from a ministerial team made up of two advocates, a PR man and an insurance broker, all once dependent on the squabbles, vanities and mortality of the rest of us, for a living. Any dearth of entrepreneurship in modern Scotland is, I'm convinced, a deeply complex phenomenon.

For three years now, week in week out, I've been visiting a wide variety of Scotland's unquoted growth companies, talking to the people who make them tick and writing longish Saturday profiles about them. That experience has given me a perspective on the question at issue here. But, as a journalist, I'm only too aware that, in seeking a real diagnosis for Scotland's apparent

*Jimmy Gulliver at
Edinburgh Airport,
1986.*

*David Murray
surveys his kingdom,
Ibrox, Glasgow,
1988.*

lack of enterprise, I may be reduced to yet another assemblage of boardroom tit-bits. Which Scottish company chairman was once an activist in the Workers' Revolutionary Party but prefers yachting these days; who carries home the fattest pay cheque; or drives the fastest Ferrari? That sort of thing. But if we are to answer David Murray's insistent question, we must identify what differentiates that rare bird, the young Scottish entrepreneur, from the rest of us. And if, in our search, we blunder into gossip from time to time, the fault is all mine.

Entrepreneur is one of those words still in transit across our linguistic landscape. When it was first absorbed, in the 1880s, it meant the manager of a musical institution, a provider of entertainment. Quickly it came to connote any intermediary between labour and capital. But it was only in its second century in the English language, in the 'Greed is Good' 1980s, that entrepreneur took on a steelier edge, becoming the portmanteau term for a profit-driven deal-doer, this year building businesses, next year asset-stripping someone else's creation, depending on which approach best feeds the bottom line.

So why do so few Scots nowadays become entrepreneurs? Are we too nice? Too cossetted by a mother hen state to enjoy the risks? Too collectivist in our instincts to participate in a business for driven individualists? Is the culture more to blame than the human raw material, impelling what those left at home would see as Scots on the make to realise their dreams far from their native land?

As our starting point, let's take a closer look at that raw material. Entrepreneurs, it seems to me, come in two sub-species. There are those, like Ian Wood and former Olympic pole-vaulter David Stevenson, who took existing family businesses and breathed new life into them. Wood turned the fishing business his grandfather had founded in Aberdeen into a diversified oil services group, exploiting, more than most locals, the offshore opportunities on his own doorstep. Stevenson brought retailing flair to the family textiles business in Langholm, expanding the highly successful Edinburgh Woollen Mill chain of knitwear shops.

Both men are worthy of the entrepreneur tag. But they had a family culture to imbibe and something to work with. The really fascinating entrepreneurs, for my money, are the ones who created a business empire out of nothing. Men like Sir Norman Macfarlane, who, over four decades, built up a mini-conglomerate based on packaging, now capitalised at £82 million, but started, legend has it, with a £200 gratuity after military service. Or David Murray, who was to be found, in his teens, doing up room-and-kitchens in Duns and selling them on at a profit, and now harbours the ambition of creating the largest private business empire in the country. Rags to riches is probably an overstatement, but this group is surely a purer sample of the species.

While not inheriting a family business, some of this breed do come from entrepreneurial backgrounds. Murray's father was a successful coal merchant in Ayr, who sent his son to Fettes, but lost everything gambling on the horses. The McNeil brothers, who created Apollo, the window blind manufacturer and franchised retail network – sold on last year for an astonishing £54.8 million – had a father who started keeping mink in a Glasgow back-court and went on to become the biggest mink farmer in the UK, in Aberdeenshire.

Louis Goodman, who has built City Site Estates into a significant, listed property company in less than a decade, started the business in the backroom of his mother's dress shop in Glasgow's Glassford Street. Ivor Tiefenbrun,

David Stevenson, spinning his family fortune, Langholm, 1983.

You can't get better than a . . . Tom Farmer, Edinburgh, 1986.

scourge of bureaucracies and manufacturer of a Rolls Royce range of hi-fi equipment, comes from a family which already ran a sub-contract precision engineering business.

There are others – like Tom Farmer, the garage hand who created the Kwik-Fit tyre and exhaust depot chain; Gerard Eadie, the replacement window king; and George Simpson, the Aberdonian behind the Craigendarroch hotel, leisure and timeshare concept – who have come to business success entirely by their own efforts. But they, in my experience, are as rare as sea eagles on our corporate landscape.

The really striking characteristic which differentiates most of our freestanding entrepreneurs is how small a part formal education appears to have played in their development. Murray, who was withdrawn from Fettes and sent to Broughton High when the last of his father's money was in the bookmakers' grasp, was more of a playground trader than a committed scholar, admitting to reading only two books in his life – George Orwell's *Animal Farm* and *The Slater Walker Story*. Brian Souter who, with his older sister Ann, has created Perth-based Stagecoach, the biggest private bus operator in Britain, flirted briefly with an accountancy career, but was always drawn to the buses which his father had driven and where he was to be found conducting in his spare time, when he should have been totting up other people's columns of figures.

Brian Gilda, the young man who has spread his People's Ford dealership from unpromising beginnings in recession-hit Bathgate out as far away as Liverpool, left school at 15 and has not, so far, needed to look back. I heard Wallace Mercer, the wealthy property developer and chairman of Heart of Midlothian Football Club, on the radio the other day, recalling that when he left Eastwood High School, one teacher warned him that he was destined to be one of life's hewers of wood and drawers of water.

Of course such anecdotal evidence is not decisive. Other entrepreneurs, particularly those who have inherited a family business, have enjoyed high-level, often expensive, educations. Fraser Morrison, who recently bought back control of the family construction business his father founded in Tain after the war, is an engineering graduate of Edinburgh University. David Erdal (Glenalmond, Oxford, Harvard and the WRP) has not found his pedigree an obstacle in expanding the family papermaking business, Tullis Russell of Markinch, into one of Europe's largest independents. An older breed of Scottish entrepreneurs, men like Jimmy Gulliver and Sir Ian MacGregor, had distinguished terms at university.

But it is surely more than coincidence that so many of Scotland's young entrepreneurs (particularly the self-starters) have relied more on native intuition, drive and a dash or two of luck to create their chances than any clutch of Highers or college degrees. Our cherished education system, regarded by generations of Scots as the highway along which their children must travel to find self-improvement, has produced conformist pressures which seem to militate against risk-taking. The spread of formal business education has concentrated on management skills, not entrepreneurship.

Today, the white-haired Sir Norman Macfarlane – multi-millionaire, arts patron, cleanser of the Guinness stable, occasional golfing partner for Denis Thatcher – is a pillar of the Scottish establishment. But they say that the sight of the young Macfarlane, delivering, in person, the paper bags and stationery, even the follow-up invoices, to his early customers, raised many a disdainful guffaw at the local rugby club. The fellow was in trade, after all. And everyone knew that the way to get on in life was a solid degree and a career in law, accountancy or medicine.

Taking both sides . . . Gerard Eadie, 1987.

The hegemony of the professions is now showing some signs of cracking, thank God. Perhaps more lawyers and accountants have come to realise that their fee notes are earned, in considerable measure, on the back of the entrepreneurial effort of others. But the education system still seems curiously unsure about what, if anything, it can contribute to the revival of our industrial and commercial base. That revival, meanwhile, such as it is, has often flourished on some very unpromising academic soil.

If you doubt the uncanny correlation between entrepreneurial success and academic failure, consider another remarkable feature of Scotland's thin ranks of post-war business builders; the significant number of immigrants among them, who have had to pick their way through our national idiosyncrasies and our language to realise their business dreams.

I recall the tireless rates campaigner and Glasgow financier, Bill Mann, telling me why he decided to back an Italian immigrant, Gio Benedetti, who wanted to start an industrial laundry in Ayrshire. Mann, one of whose achievements is the revival of Glasgow's Western Baths Club, was tempted to do what no other bank would do, partly because Benedetti had just swum right round the Island of Cumbrae. His faith was amply justified. The young Italian went on to create a business with more than 2,000 industrial customers all over the UK, which he sold, in 1988, to BET for £13.5 million.

Benedetti is a recent example of a well-established trend. Sir Reo Stakis, who arrived from Cyprus in 1942, opened one small restaurant in Glasgow, and went on to build it into a hotels, leisure and healthcare group. Or Yaqub Ali, who fled to Scotland in the 1950s and created Castle, the Gorbals-based cash-and-carry warehouse which today claims to be the biggest in Europe.

There are plenty of other contemporary examples, like Henk van Eck, the imposing Dutchman who picked the Clydesdale electrical retailing chain off the floor after an earlier buy-out went badly wrong. Or, closer to home, the English couple, Pat and Alex Grant, who showed that you could make money manufacturing domestic freezers in far-flung Caithness. Or Bristol-born Geoff Ball, who turned the prosaically-named City of Aberdeen Land Association into CALA, the up-market housebuilder whose formula many have since tried to copy.

So, if immigrants and academic drop-outs can stir Scotland's modest entrepreurial pot, what other factors are inhibiting the rest of the natives? I've already touched on the lure of the professions, but there are other aspects of our educational and cultural values which seem, to me, to be antipathetic to unbridled individual enterprise.

The converse of our traditional veneration of formal education is a besetting fear of failure. In Silicon Valley in California, in the trading maelstroms of Hong Kong or Taiwan, businesses are born and die all the time. Failure, particularly in America, is treated as something to chalk up against experience, not as a badge of dishonour.

We, too, have our crop of entrepreurial failures. Brian Palmer, a Liverpudlian, was threatening to turn Hinari, his home entertainments manufacturing business, into another Amstrad. Instead his tight-margin, high-volume business went bust. Ian Littlewood, a former communications technician with Lothian and Borders Police, made GL Group one of the corporate phenomena of the 1980s. Fast cars, a company plane and offices for the home security division which were said to have a control room which could withstand a nuclear attack. The mess left behind when the whole thing collapsed is still rumbling through the courts.

Others could be added to the list. Like Frank Lafferty, the Glasgow Builder. Or Derek Diamond, the bridge-playing Glaswegian, whose mechanical

Gio Benedetti on Irvine Beach, 1988.

breakdown insurance empire was taken to the Stock Market, only to have the shares suspended six months later, in circumstances which have still to be made clear.

Every time a Scots entrepreneur hits the wall, there seems to be a determination to poke around the circumstances of his or her demise, on the assumption that something shady has been going on. Now, I would be the first to concede that there is sometimes dirt to be found. But there are honest failures too. And our obsession with the murkier side of commercial downfalls simply reinforces our collective fear of failing. And that, I suspect, means that fewer people will run the risk in the first place.

Most entrepreneurs are driven, in part, by a powerful desire to make a lot more money than the next guy. And that again, I suspect, limits the culture of enterprise in Scotland. I am not arguing that Scots are wealth-averse. But there are significant constraints, in our culture, on wanting too much or flaunting what you have too openly. Successful Scottish entrepreneurs are prone to sell-out when they can get £5 million or £10 million for their business. Few seem interested in becoming mega-rich. At a more modest level, most Scottish business executives on £50,000 a year, say, think they've arrived anyway. As an added bonus, they can measure quality of life in how few minutes it takes them to get on the golf course. Most see no need to risk it all by starting their own venture.

Even if they have felt the itch, the corporate structures in which many of our managers work are not the best environments for breeding entrepreneurs. So much of the Scottish industry is now either externally controlled or the result of direct inward investment. We suffer from the branch plant syndrome, with many of our major industries run by line managers whose authority and discretion are carefully prescribed by group HQ in London, Boston or Tokyo. One subtle side-effect of that loss of local control is the way it alters the prevailing management culture and smothers the kind of initiative needed to strike out on your own.

The picture is not unrelieved gloom. There are interesting new players emerging in sectors like publishing, the hotel and restaurant trade, healthcare and computer software development. Some can prosper happily in a domestic market of little more than five million people. But the more specialist concerns immediately have to think exports if they intend to become serious players. The Japanese and the emerging Little Tiger economies on the Pacific Rim have taught us you can export anything from cars to compact disc players around the globe.

But they don't have the shadow of Knox and Calvin on their backs, nor the heavy weight of an educational system which continues to instil fear of failure, dogging their endeavours. More of them are hungry, too, just like our forebears.

Reo Stakis, Glasgow,
1983.

Wallace Mercer
plans the future,
Tynecastle,
Edinburgh, 1990.

Glen Etive, 1950.

*Tayfuirst village,
Glencoe, 1951.*

JOHN FOWLER

Weird Peaks and a
Myriad Lochans

The Mountains of Scotland

'I TO THE HILLS WILL LIFT MINE EYES' SANG THE METRICAL PSALMIST.
In the year 1803 the poet and metaphysician Samuel Taylor Coleridge lifted
his eyes and recorded in his notebook: 'I went to the window, to empty
my urine-pot, & wondered at the simple grandeur of the View.' We must
all have admired the hills, chanty in hand or no. Coleridge was not merely
a window gazer, he tramped the hills too. When he paused in wonder at the
window-sill he had not long returned from a visit to the Highlands where, in
a kind of delirium, he tried to master the symptoms of opium withdrawal by a
sustained cross country pedestrian expedition in which he covered 263 miles in
eight days, an average of 33 miles a day. Coleridge was a prodigious hill walker
even when not driven by his addiction and few would try to match his exploits
now. But we can all watch from the window, as most people do, content with
the view from ground level. This is pleasing; I wouldn't sneer, though the best
views are undoubtedly from the top, gained after some exertion of wind and
limb.

W. A. Poucher, a resolute hill walker and photographer who died in 1988
at the age of 96, imagined a group of young people in Lochaber visualising
themselves 'standing by one of the summit cairns, inhaling the invigorating
mountain air and scanning the glens far below, the chain of engirdling hills
and the distant glimmering seas'. This is the ultimate reward though I'm sure
that Poucher, even at his purplest (in this case in his well-thumbed book *The
Scottish Peaks*) would want to make the implicit proviso that such treats
are a bonus and the days of wide and wondrous views are rare. On more
common days little may be seen but the moist grey features of the immediate
surroundings and the dim outline of the next slope glimpsed momentarily
through mist. Driving rain and snarling winds are frequent companions on
the Scottish hills.

Hills? Mountains? Who can define what a mountain is and what
distinguishes it from lesser neighbours? In mere height measured above
sea level the Scottish mountains may seem paltry compared to Alpine or
Pyrenean peaks and mere dwarfs alongside the giants of the Caucasus or
the Rockies or Andes, let alone the Himalayas. The stony grandeur of Ben
Nevis has less altitude than the grassy tops of minor Alpine outliers in, say,
Provence. Yet Scotland's high hills are truly mountainous, a claim validated
both by the experience of climbers able to make the comparison with other
countries and by the simple evidence of tourist eyes.

The dictionaries are little help. Chambers contents itself with defining
mountain as 'a high hill'. The *Shorter OED* is wordier but not clearer: 'A
natural elevation of the earth's surface, rising notably above the surrounding
level.' Doctor Johnson's lexicon allows a choice between a 'large hill' and 'a
vast protuberance of the earth'.

Simple yardsticks are treacherous. You might, for example, take Munro's
tables as a rough and ready guide to what constitutes a mountain. Almost a
century ago Sir Hugh Munro was delegated by the Scottish Mountaineering

Club to ascertain the number of Scottish peaks of 3,000 feet or more. Many people were astonished to learn when he produced his list that it contained a sum total of nearly 280. Later juggling has lopped a few from the list and added a few more, giving a grand total of 277 at the last count. But the Munro is an abstract idea rather than an incontrovertible natural feature, an approximation dreamed up by the statisticians in which a mountain is defined not merely by height but by such matters as the rise and fall between distinct peaks, so that the definition of a Munro is almost as much a matter of subjective judgement as simple measurement. Once documented, however, the Munros have proved a lure to ardent hill walkers. Sir Hugh measured but didn't scale them all; he left two unclimbed at his death, though even before that a man of the cloth, the Revd A. E. Roberts had conquered them all after a 'desultory campaign' lasting ten years. His formidable figure late in life is pictured in the Scottish Mountaineering Club's book *The Munros* (a bible for walkers); slouched on the thwart of a ferry on its way to the Hebrides, his white hair topped by a Glengarry bonnet, and beside him his jut-chinned lady of equally indomitable aspect. Since then the trickle of Munroists has grown to a flood; Hamish Brown knocked off the lot in one four-month route march in 1978 and has completed the circuit several times since. Hundreds of aspirants are ticking off the mountain tops in emulation at this moment.

God gave us the mountains and not even Sir Hugh Munro and the SMC shall categorise them. Simple rule of thumb is no help. The Cobbler, a surreal caracole of rock at the head of Loch Long, is too lowly to qualify as a Munro and yet it is the dominant, most attractive and most challenging hill in the so-called Arrochar Alps. Neither the Torridian sandstone stump of Stac Pollaidh in the barren moorland north of Ullapool, nor Goat Fell, the symmetrical arrowhead of the Arran peaks, is a Munro, but both are mountains in the eye of the beholder even if they fall short of the magic 3,000 feet, or its duller metrical equivalent, 914 metres.

Some, like Stac Pollaidh or the elegant conic hill Schiehallion, stand alone, visible and immediately identifiable from far and wide because of the lie of the land; but single peaks in a plain are the exception. The rugged buttresses that rise dramatically from Glen Coe lead upwards to summits more or less of a height; they are the glaciated skeletal bones of a huge massif gouged and scooped by the ice cap in its retreat. Such, too, are the Cairngorms. Climb to the weather station on the bouldery hump of Cairn Gorm itself and southwards in undulating folds stretches a great plateau; that knob on a seemingly insignificant rise some three miles to the south-west is the trig point atop Ben Macdui, not much more than a pimple though it crowns the second highest mountain in the country. Seen from the summits, the mountain ranges roll to the horizon like waves of a petrified sea. Yet even in the midst of these choppy land masses the practised eye will pick out salient features. Easily recognised among the hills around Crianlarich are the twin peaks of Ben More (one of many given that name) and Stob Binein; the Ben a perfect cone, Binein sliced askew on the crest. Southwards, Ben Lomond stands proud, sharper than you would imagine from the familiar sidelong view across the loch. Unmistakeable, too, is the hunched shoulder of Ben Nevis, too ponderous to be pretty, and the familiar tipsy saw-edge of the Cruachan cirque above Loch Awe.

Topographically, the mountains of Scotland divide into homogenous groups with certain broad characteristics. Not all mountains are Highland hills. South of the flat industrial corridor between Glasgow and Edinburgh are the green whalebacks of the Lowther and Moffat hills, and more rugged, barren terrain in Galloway, where, within picnicking distance of Glen Trool, the neglected Merrick rises to a modest, tawny 843 metres, making it the highest peak in the south of Scotland. Spreading northwards between Glasgow and the western reaches of the Caledonian Canal are several clusters of craggy mountains; the Arrochar Alps, and the big mountains of successively Glen Etive, Glencoe, the Black Mount and the remoter hills on the northern fringes of the wild, water-speckled Moor of Rannoch. Ben Nevis and its paladins guard the way to the far north, and between them and the Glen Coe hills rise the shapely Mamores (the name means breasts). The engineer James Watt, visiting the north to survey a route for the Caledonian Canal described these western mountains thus: 'The Highland mountains, which commence at the Firth of Clyde, extend upon the west side of the Country to the Northernmost Parts of Scotland; in general they begin close at the Sea shore; they are intersected by deep but narrow Vallies: the Quantity of Arable Land is exceeding small, and its Product greatly lessened by the prodigious rains that fall upon the Coast. The tops of the Mountains are craggy, and their Sides are steep, but they produce a Grass very proper for breeding small Black Cattle, and in some Places for feeding Sheep.' Black cattle apart, gone from these pastures along with the drovers of a past age, the description will stand for today.

Eastwards, in the massy uplands bounded by the A9 over the high, bleak Pass of Drumochter, and the fertile plains of Deeside, are the Cairngorms. Strictly speaking the name applies only to part of the larger range more properly called the Grampians, as in the geography books (or in Home's leaden tragedy *Douglass* – 'My name is Norval,' declaims its young hero. 'On the Grampian Hills my father feeds his flock'). The true Cairngorms boast a clutch of huge hills more than 1,200 metres in height, a tableland capped by Cairn Gorm, Ben Macdui, Braeriach and Cairn Toul, four of the five highest hills in the country. This is a wild land; calculated to please the cross-country skier in winter and early spring; treeless and – once the plateau is gained – apparently featureless, though closer inspection discovers that it is riven by chasms, corries, gullies and sheer cliffs where tough ice climbing is on offer in winter. The inhospitable Lairig Ghru pass bisects this high, windswept wilderness.

North of the Caledonian Canal there are distinctive groups of remote mountains – in Kintail; in the barren sea-moated 'rough bounds' of Knoydart; in Torridon, whose sandstone hills are white-capped even in summer – but with quartzite rock, not snow; and in the north-west where weird peaks overlook a land riddled and pocked with a myriad tiny lochans and watercourses. Offshore, mountains spring from many of the Western Isles, notably the Cuillins of Skye, 'a prodigious range of mountains capped with rocky pinnacles in a strange variety of shapes', in the words of James Boswell, who saw them on his travels with Dr Johnson. Boswell looked on mountains with a kindlier eye than his companion; while the biographer might appreciate a 'grand prospect of the rude mountains of Moidart and Knoidart', his urbane companion much preferred gentler views: 'An eye accustomed to flowery pastures and waving harvests is astonished and repelled by this wide extent of hopeless sterility,' he opined. The tops of the Cuillins are not easily gained by the casual walker and many of its slopes defy all but the skilled mountaineer. Some Cuillins rock has the dismaying property of disorienting the magnetic compass.

Scotland's mountain bedrock – granite, basalt, gneiss, gabbro, mica-schist, quartz and quartzite are some common ingredients – can be a happy hunting ground for the amateur geologist. Slate was quarried until recent years at

WEIRD PEAKS
AND A
MYRIAD
LOCHANS

178

*Zero Gully, Ben
Nevis.*

*The mountains of
Lochaber on the
north side of Glen
Nevis.*

Ballachulish, near Glencoe, and mineral deposits include even some gold, now being worked again as a pilot commercial project in Ben Chuirn, a lesser companion of Ben Lui, near Tyndrum.

By and large the Scottish hills are bare of trees; 'What is not heath is nakedness,' as Johnson observed. Two centuries later his comment is still true, though it was not always the case. In old times these slopes were thickly forested from glen almost to peak; oak, alder, hazel, birch and pine grew there in profusion, distributed according to soil, climate and exposure. Only vestiges remain. Large forests can still be found, especially in the east of the country, but man and the animals he introduced, namely sheep and deer, have combined to strip the old forest cover. Forests were decimated for a variety of purposes; as fuel or building material, for land clearance and for conversion to charcoal for the smelting ovens; they have even been destroyed in war as a scorched earth policy. Survival and regeneration has been impaired by grazing beasts cropping the seedlings.

Remnants of the old Caledonian Forest of Scotch pine still stand, some quite close to populous parts, like the kingly stems and dark spreading crowns that ennoble the open hillsides north of Loch Lomond on the way to Crianlarich. Other ancient woodlands survive in Deeside, where the Balmoral Forest stretches between Ballater and Braemar, and in Speyside, which has the extensive Rothiemurchus Forest. Ample evidence of a vanished environment is found all over the Highlands in the boggy moorlands where a flotsam of bleached stumps and gnarled boughs surfaces among the black peat hags. I often wonder if landowners might be persuaded to reverse the creeping decay of the native pines by planting seedlings from old stock. It would be expensive, but perhaps public funds could be made available? One attempt is being made in the glen above Barrisdale Bay on Loch Hourn, where the John Muir Trust, a body of conservationists named after the great Scots-American naturalist, has a programme for regenerating the native (indeed uniquely local) species of Scots pine. In the last 60 years widespread commercial afforestation, led by Forestry Commission planting, has reclaimed much ground for timber, while in the process daubing glens and hillsides with great patches of dark evergreen spruce. Seldom beautiful and often ugly, difficult of access, dark and virtually impenetrable, this parvenu forest is too often a poor exchange scenically for open hillscape.

But yes, Scottish hills are still very bare, with small cover over rock structure. In autumn the slopes of the eastern hills blaze with purple heather. The bracken unfurls its delicate fronds to give an ankle-snagging summer tangle underfoot. Deer grass, tawnier than the stag itself, clothes much of the upper grounds. I have been astonished in the Mamores at the intensity of its russet, red and yellows tints. Many ridges are carpeted in hair moss. Clumps of blaeberry cling to the ground and in late summer offer a small refreshment of tiny berries, blue and bloomed. On a smaller scale there are specimens of alpine and arctic plants, shy rarities to be found sheltering in rocky niches and crannies by observant naturalists. Ben Lawers on Loch Tayside, with its congenial alkaline soil, is the best known habitat of such species – indeed there is a nature trail to help visitors identify them – but they also flourish on less publicised slopes.

Alfred Wainwright, the idiosyncratic chronicler and illustrator of Lakeland fells, regretted, when he came to tackle the Scottish hills, the barbarity of their names. Gaelic at least has rules, responded Hamish Brown in his book *The Groats End Walk*. But I agree with Wainwright; compared to the yeoman simplicity of the Lake District, these Gaelic names are rebarbative. They don't trip off the tongue (unless you are aware that, for example, Laithair

Beinn is pronounced Larven). The popular hills are often anglicised but others, at least on the printed page, seem hopeless cases; taken at random you can cite A'Bhuidheanach Beag, Mullach Coire Mhic Fhearchair or Sgurr nan Ceathreamhnan. Even worse are the cumbersome names given to simple mountain streams, grand names, sometimes, for the merest dribble of water. Who names these features on the map? I suspect cartographers' whim rather than local lore, but I have no proof.

The impression is easily gained that empty upland spaces are open to all wanderers, but this is not strictly the case. Most moorland is privately owned, increasingly by business enterprises or wealthy individuals, often foreign, eager to maximise profit on their investments. The result may be a change of land use and restricted access. The recent controversy over forestry investment schemes which encouraged widespread planting in unsuitable wilderness areas for tax advantages is one example. Another is the conflict over the proposed development of skiing facilities in Lurcher's Gully in the Cairngorms, a project fiercely opposed by environmental groups. Conversely, not everyone who loves the hills and wants to protect their special features welcomes the suggested creation of national parks covering large areas of the remoter Highlands. One potential drawback of the national park idea is that it might regulate and curtail the relatively free access which walkers have long enjoyed on Scottish slopes. Freedom to roam is already limited in deer stalking areas during the late summer and early autumn months when the guns are out. Those of us who regard the wild parts of Scotland as a birthright, sanctified by custom, must be prepared to fight our case.

As Coleridge knew, the best way to appreciate the hills is to walk over them. I came to hill walking and scrambling relatively late, so I have plenty of exploring to look forward to. I have tramped the hills in all seasons; I have struggled manfully against storm-driven spindrift and plunged into sunlit rock pools. Some hills I return to again and again, either because they're close to where I live, or particularly inviting, or both. One of my first attempts, when still short of experience and wobbly on the question of navigation, took me and some equally foolhardy friends on to the wrong (that is, precipitous) side of Cruachan in thick mist, and we were lucky to come to no harm after a nervous nine hours on the hill. A year later, sweltering on a sunny day, I romped the length of the Cruachan ridge in between trains. And on a third expedition I wandered in the white silence of its snowy corniced crests.

Sheer size is unimportant; mountains don't need to be big to be enjoyed. Take tiny Ben A'n on the shores of Loch Katrine – not really a mountain at all, for it's lowly indeed. But nonetheless, it has the character of a mountain in little. It's a delight. So is the Pap of Glencoe (Sgorr na Ciche, to give it its Sunday name) which is negligible compared to its near neighbours, but from whose rocky tonsured summit one hot Sunday I enjoyed marvellous views of hill, glen, loch and sea. And while the more spectacular slopes of Glencoe were thronged, we had the Pap to ourselves.

What is it draws me to the hills? Friends find my passion strange. Coleridge knew, of course, and confided it to his friend Thomas Wedgwood (of the pottery family): 'I never find myself at one within the embracement of rocks and hills . . . but my spirit courses, drives, and eddies, like a Leaf in Autumn . . . I do not think it possible that any bodily pains could eat out the love & joy, that is so substantially part of me, towards hills, & rocks, & steep waters!'

Buchanan Street,
Glasgow, 1975.

Buchanan Street,
Glasgow, 1954.

WILLIAM RUSSELL

Envoi

The View from London

AND NOW FOR SOMETHING UTTERLY OTHERWISE. A SENTENCE, I TRUST, which did not end as anticipated and neither will this book. An *envoi* ought to sum up all that has gone before, but I have no idea what has gone before, except that it was the inmates' view of the asylum. Instead, therefore, here is the view from the outside looking in.

After 25 years in London, Scotland has become for me in many ways Another Country. But it is not a foreign country. Down in England I remain a Scot. Here my accent is as clear as a bell, even if nobody can pinpoint the part of Scotland from which I come – all Scottish accents sound the same to non-Scots, particularly the English.

Up in Scotland, however, it is regarded as having been corrupted, anglicised perhaps, pan loaf certainly, and suspect indubitably. Nationalists decree that someone living outside the ghetto cannot really understand Scotland, which is arrant nonsense. It might conceivably be true, were I an exile in the strict sense, but the umbilical cord has never been cut. I have always worked for the *Glasgow Herald*, and have been deeply involved in things Scottish, albeit at Westminster, for much of the time. All those politicians, from John Rankin to George Foulkes, Winifred to Margaret Ewing, David Steel to David Steel, and Michael Clark Hutchison to Malcolm Rifkind, the sublime to the ridiculous to the mentally insufficient – politicians are not usually completely barking mad – saw to that.

The point about being on the outside looking in at where one came from is that one has a sense of detachment about what one sees, rather like one of those intrepid Scots teaplanters who, after years in Assam waited on hand and foot, returns home to a bungalow in Bridge of Allan, Dunblane or Moffat to find that things are not only not what they were, but worse. Such folk do not like the changes, but they recognise the place, and understand the society.

At the same time, working for the *Herald* has meant I have felt none of that peculiar necessity to preserve my Scottishness, which afflicts so many London Scots. I do not cling to ways nobody back home still follows, feel no need to belong to Home Counties Caledonian societies, attend Welsh Burns suppers or loup around in a kilt at East Anglian Scottish country dancing classes.

Coming home is always a surprise, because there is inevitably something new amidst the familiar faces and places. Sometimes the discovery delights, occasionally it saddens. Take Buchanan Street on a sunny Saturday afternoon, for instance. At first pedestrianisation was a sad affair for anybody reared in the days when it rang with the clanging of the trams, and was lined with great shops, the match of anything London could offer, where mannequins paraded to the clatter of teacups and the floor walkers talked Kelvinside. But it has come through the doldrums of a decade ago, risen from the slough, and is now a bustling precinct in which street entertainers, who sound every bit as good as those one used to see topping the bill at the Pavilion or the Metropole, or at the bottom of the bill at the Alhambra, vie for the attention of the crowds. True, the great stores are but a shadow of themselves, the Argyle Arcade no

longer reeks of class, and the splendidly pompous *Herald* office is no more. But things are thriving and, after the years of dereliction, the great crystal palace of the St Enoch Square development across Argyll Street comes as a thrill. Maybe it contains the same old mix of chain stores and franchises common to every shopping centre from John o'Groats to Land's End, but the building itself is a joyful place, a cathedral of commerce, every bit as worth boasting about as the over-lauded building which houses the Burrell Collection – overkill on which has long since occurred – or that apple of the Duke of Rothesay's eye, Princes Square.

And then there is the Central Station. Once the finest of the stations built in the great age of the steam train with its wonderful boards setting out the destinations to Clyde Coast resorts with names as mysterious, remote and glamorous as any place in Cathay or Khatmandhu, it became for a while a clapped-out, dirty, dosser's paradise. Then suddenly, or so it seemed, it was gloriously revived, a concourse of shops was created in the style of the old facades where the destination boards once hung, and the space beneath the glass roof was transformed from a filthy concrete wasteland to a gleaming marble piazza. It became what a station ought to be, a place in which to linger, to encounter, to relish. London has nothing so fine. From down here it is clear that Scotland's cities are not in crisis, whatever difficulties they face. London, grinding to a halt, is a dirty, violent, unhappy, expensive place. Maybe that fate lies ahead for some Scots cities, and one cannot ignore Edinburgh's drug problem, with its associated Aids cases. But it is still nothing like as bad as it is here.

At times from down here, Scotland looks like it is trying to turn itself into one great theme park for the benefit of the tourists, and while civic pride is admirable it really does depend on being proud of something worth the effort. Back home in Lanark last year, I noted with amazement on the wall of one back lane a handsome plaque announcing this was a conservation area consecrated by the Civic Trust. The people in that very Trust had spent their youth trying to get the hell out of lanes like that, as had their parents. All they wanted, when we were all young, was to have it knocked down as quickly as possible, which was always the Scottish way with buildings that had outlived their usefulness.

Living up a close, however, is now smart, provided it is in that phoniest of Glasgow estate agents' creations, the Merchant City, or its equivalent. The resuscitated buildings look fine, but there is a dangerous whiff of preciousness. These were once streets of commerce, of power; then they became mean streets down which a brave man ventured seldom, and never after dark; today, however, the Jocks and Nigels, the Fionas and Shionas run rampant from wine bar to wine bar in their Giorgio Armani style clothes, worn, it has to be said, without style, parking the Porsche with impunity.

The great Scottish tradition used to be, when a thing was done, knock it down and put up something new. Building was functional, met the need of the moment. That was why, in spite of growing up in the second oldest royal burgh in the land, I grew up surrounded by houses of no great antiquity. An equivalent English town would have had Georgian terraces, Elizabethan cottages, Jacobean manor houses, Victorian villas, something from pretty well every period, cosetted and pampered, and once the Civic Trust had arrived, painted in pretty pastels. Our buildings were either old and decrepit, or new and neat and tidy, but they were never architecturally worth bothering about. Now they have plaques on them, and yesterday' slums are today's craft centres. New Lanark is a case in point. A damp, decaying village buried in a gorge on the banks of the Clyde, it is now a centre where tourists

Wemyss Bay queue, Central Station, Glasgow, 1954.

can buy goods that no Scot ever owned, wanted, used or consumed in his life. A dump is a dump whatever is done to it.

Then there is the food. I first discovered bashed neeps and champit tatties on a taste of Scotland menu. As for those puddings made from oatmeal and cream, pure fiction from start to finish. All this is part of the tourist culture which threatens the real thing. From down here Scotland also displays a mind-boggling lack of sophistication. That dreadful culture-year slogan, Glasgowing on, printed in fake Rennie Mackintosh script, is but the tip of a monstrously large iceberg whose other triumphs range from the gruesome Costa Clyde, coined in a bid to keep the locals from going to Benidorm by pretending there was an equally jolly 'costa' back home, to Glasgow Smiles Better – than the advertising, sniped the graffiti artist. A perfect example of what I mean is provided by the current television culture-year arts magazine, *Saturday Night Clyde*, a title which is surely one of the worst imaginable, a pun on a pun smacking of the provincial at its most banal. From down here Scotland at times is just that, provincial in the worst sense.

In other ways, however, things have changed for the better. Back in the days of Old Basso Profundo, Willie Ross, one of the most effective opposition spokesmen the Labour Party ever had, Scots seemed to be forever whingeing, holding out the begging bowl, rather like too many Scots today who clutter up the doorways in the Strand asking passers-by for change. In truth the bowl was usually rather well-filled, although there was a lot to complain about. Our heavy industries were dying, and what we were given in their place did not thrive. Maybe we should have complained less and done more for ourselves at the time, because what we are seeing today could be said to be the inevitable result of all that greetin'. Ravenscraig was always doomed. Better perhaps to have faced up to that years ago.

Today there is no sense of moaning minnies prevailing. From down here one gets the feeling of a people who are at last doing something about things for themselves: there is a vitality in the air which used to be noticeable by its absence. Heavens above, can it be that the Scots are really Britain's only true Thatcherites? Or is it just that they have learned to be pragmatic? After all, Strathclyde works remarkably well, a living, breathing pragmatism success story. The Scottish health service works, maybe not perfectly, but from down here it looks like the promised land where the halt, the elderly and the disadvantaged get help. Trains are cleaner, streets are safer, licensing hours are more civilised, drunks far less trouble, and restaurants, when they are not faking tastes of Scotland, a delicious surprise, not least when the bill arrives. And how nice it is to be served by a fellow Scot, not some pepperpot-wielding Latin, or mutinous Carribean seeing racial insults in every gesture, sometimes with reason. Waitresses in black dresses and white aprons who call one 'Son' persist in spite of the blight of MacDonalds.

As for the policemen, they are infinitely politer than any encountered down here. One of the amazing things about the Turnberry Summit was that, in spite of the appalling weather, the police, doomed to hang around in draughty portacabins or parade round the links with their dogs in the rain and wind, remained so affable and pleased to talk. In London, in the South-East, virtually anywhere in England, they would have been surly, abusive, hostile, provocative, longing to put the boot in.

Just as drinking habits are better, Scots football fans no longer seem like one of the seven plagues of Israel. There was a time when a Scotland–England game at Wembley sent we exiles to the hills, our faces hidden in shame, while the tartan army laid waste the streets. Now they are good-humoured, harmless – well, almost – and rarely fighting-drunk, if seldom sober.

'Waitresses in black dresses and white aprons who call one "Son" ' – Cooper's Tea Room, Ingram Street, Glasgow, 1950.

*The concourse,
Central Station,
Glasgow, 1986.*

*Fair holiday crowds
at Central Station,
Glasgow, 1960s.*

Just after I was asked about the view from down here, I caught a television programme about novelist politicians, which quoted the passage from Disraeli's *Sybil* which Conservatives use as a bedrock of their philosophy. Even Mrs Thatcher goes on about one nation when she feels like it. I had never read the book – neither, I suspect, have many of the Tories who trumpet the slogans about 'one nation' come election time – which was remiss. Journalists, like historians, should go back to the primary source, not rely on secondary materials. So here it is.

ENVOI

'Well, society may be in its infancy,' said Egremont slightly smiling, 'but say what you like, our Queen reigns over the greatest nation that ever existed.'

'Which nation?' asked the younger stranger, 'for she reigns over two.'

The stranger paused; Egremont was silent, but looked inquiringly. 'Yes,' resumed the younger stranger after a moment's interval. 'Two nations between whom there is no intercourse and no sympathy; who are as ignorant of each other's habits, thoughts and feelings, as if they were dwellers on different zones or inhabitants on different planets; who are formed by a different breeding, are fed by a different food, are ordered by different manners, and are not governed by the same laws.'

'You speak of – ' said Egremont, hesitatingly.

'The rich and the poor.'

That last line should, of course, be 'The Scots and the English.'

A quarter of a century ago it was every young person's dream to come to London. Scotland was a place to get out of, escape committees were the order of the day. No longer. Come up home and marvel at the tidiness of it all, at the handsome suburbs with their stone-built semi-detached villas and the line upon line of bungalows, at the lack of the all-pervasive net curtain behind which the English lurk. The atmosphere is not of wealth, or self-satisfaction, but of thrift, and making do.

From down here the most striking thing is that this is a cohesive society. Everybody does not know everybody else. Scotland is not that wee. But the chances are your auntie knows somebody who knows somebody else's auntie.

Once upon a time one came home with food parcels, bearing the loot of the delicatessens of Soho to cheer up the folk back home deprived of olive oil, French cheeses, aromatic vinegars or herbs. Now one need not bother. It is all there in any High Street supermarket, and not much more expensive either. About the only thing that is noticeably different is that the vegetables are less fresh out of season. Some things are not what they used to be, others still what they used to be.

Somebody writing to our letters page took offence at a Radio Clyde advertisement for the comedienne, Victoria Wood, in which she urged her listeners to 'Eat up your neeps, pop on your kilts and hop on a tram'. But the fat lady who sings had a point, had spotted one of the things that from down here can appal, the way we wallow in nostalgia. I still reel from the broadside on our letters page aimed at me when I stated the obvious about Lanark's status as a royal and ancient borough, which is that it has not got it any longer. Royal boroughs were units of local government, nothing more, nothing less. When the unit ceases to function it is daft to cling to the status. It is meaningless. It is not daft to honour the tradition, and, like lots of small towns swallowed up by local government changes, the admirable thing is the way Lanark's sense of community has survived. That is what ought to be celebrated, not a long-outdated administrative status.

The curse of this nostalgia is easily seen from the contents of the brochures

Scottish football fans in London, 1977.

London Scots bring in the New Year outside St Paul's Cathedral, London, 1921.

shoved out by the Scottish Tourist Board, and from the contents of the bookstall at Glasgow Airport. Why on earth is *No Mean City* on sale? It is about time we burnt that book, or at least consigned it to the dustbin of literary history, along with all those foggy, out-of-focus, black-and-white photographs of Glasgow's tenements or Edinburgh's Royal Mile. As for the myth about the audience, first house Glasgow Empire, Heaven knows there hasn't been a Glasgow Empire in decades and variety has been dead even longer.

The truth, however, is that whatever the problems, the grass is now truly greener on your side of the fence. It may not look like it to you, but that was ever the way about the greenness of grass. I can assure you it is. Much, much greener.

Notes on Contributors

ARNOLD KEMP, son of the distinguished playwright and novelist Robert Kemp, has been editor of the *Herald* since 1981. He received a traditional bourgeois education at Edinburgh Academy and Edinburgh University, but the raffish side of his persona soon surfaced in an abiding addiction to jazz and the Hibernian Football Club. His other interests include cycling and the theatre. He is one of the few living Scots who actually read the novels of Sir Walter Scott for pleasure.

HARRY REID has been deputy editor of the *Herald* since 1983. He was born in Glasgow, brought up in Aberdeen (his favourite place in all the world) and educated in Edinburgh and Oxford. He is a voracious reader of Victorian novels and American thrillers. He also enjoys studying maps, hillwalking and exploring the byways of Britain. He is married to Julie Davidson (qv) and they have a daughter, Catherine.

ANNE SIMPSON was born, and spent the early years of her life, in Dublin. She is currently writing a celebration of that city, which will succeed Glasgow as European City of Culture, for Mainstream. After her early career with the *Yorkshire Post* she moved to Glasgow in the 1970s to revive the *Herald*'s women's pages, which she did to spectacular effect. She is now the paper's chief assistant editor and also its fashion editor. Her interests include both the cinema and the theatre.

JULIE DAVIDSON is the *Herald*'s award-winning TV critic. She is also a distinguished freelance travel writer, and a regular presenter of television's *What the Papers Say*. Born in Lanarkshire, she was brought up in North Berwick and Aberdeen. She has worked in all four of Scotland's principal cities. She lists her main recreations as travelling, reading, walking – and lunching. She is married to Harry Reid (qv).

WILLIAM HUNTER is the possessor of the most original writing style in British journalism: uniquely spare and bittersweet. A Paisley man, he inevitably, and lugubriously, supports St Mirren. He wrote the commentary for Mainstream's selection from the Outram photo archives, *Dear Happy Ghosts*. In a long and fecund career with the *Herald* he has been diarist, leader writer, business editor and columnist. He also writes a column for the *Scottish Field*.

ALLAN LAING, of whom it has been said 'he is about as funny as a burning orphanage', was born and brought up in Ayrshire. His first job was as a greenkeeper at Turnberry Golf Course, the highlight of which was being hit by a ball struck by Paul Newman. He dabbled briefly (a week) with a career in the Foreign Office until they discovered that diplomacy was not his strong point. He then worked on Scottish weekly newspapers before joining the *Herald* in 1974, and has never looked forward.

JACK McLEAN, variously known as the Urban Voltaire, the Jack of all Tirades, and the Talleyrand of Toryglen, is without doubt Scotland's most controversial journalist. He was previously a teacher in the Queen's Park area of Glasgow. He started his remarkable journalistic career writing extraordinarily serious articles for the *Times Scottish Educational Supplement*, articles which gave little indication of the pyrotechnics which were to come later. His iconoclastic column and features in the *Herald* have gained him many awards. He is currently writing his autobiography.

LESLEY DUNCAN was brought up in Troon. She is that rare journalist, one who is equally skilled as a page designer and as a writer. She writes excellent poetry, about which she is unduly modest. She is currently design editor of the *Herald*'s *Weekender* section. She is married to the *Herald*'s night editor, John Duncan, and they have a son, David. She is a graduate of Glasgow University.

JOHN LINKLATER was born in Dumfries, the son of the late Allie Linklater, Shetland storyteller. He was educated at the Royal High School, Edinburgh, Stirling University and Glasgow University. He has been on the staff of the *Herald* since 1978. He was for several years the paper's education correspondent and he launched *Education Herald* in 1984. In 1987 he was seconded for six months to the *Baltimore Sun*. In 1988 he was appointed the *Herald*'s literary editor.

JACK WEBSTER, born and bred in Maud, Aberdeenshire, has had a notable career as a feature writer and editorial executive on several Scottish newspapers. He has recently developed a secondary career in television, making three acclaimed documentaries about the North-East for BBC Scotland. He has written several books, and his updated history of Aberdeen Football Club, *The Dons*, was recently published. He is currently writing the official biography of Alistair MacLean. Each of his three sons is a journalist. He joined the *Herald* in 1985.

MURRAY RITCHIE has used his trenchant Monday commentary in the *Herald* to make himself one of Scotland's most authoritative journalists. His passions include folk music and golf. He was educated at Glasgow High School. After a stint on the *Daily Record*, and four years in Kenya, he joined the *Herald* almost 20 years ago. He has since travelled the world for the paper.

JIM HEWITSON, a Glaswegian who was brought up and educated in Clydebank, was a news desk executive for the *Herald* in both Glasgow and Edinburgh. Then he and his family opted for a less complex lifestyle in Papa Westray, one of the Orkneys. He writes a monthly column about his experiences in the islands for the *Herald*. He also writes children's books.

DEREK DOUGLAS is a Borderer, born and bred. A key member of the *Herald*'s Edinburgh team, he combines news desk duties with investigative journalism. He compiled *The Flowering of Scotland* – the book that Mainstream published within four weeks of Scotland's Grand Slam triumph, and which gave the lie to the suggestion that 'quicky' books are trashy. He was co-author of the *Unfriendly Games*, another Mainstream book.

DOUGLAS DUNN was born in Inchinnan. He is one of Scotland's finest living poets and his major literary awards include the Geoffrey Faber Memorial Prize, the Hawthornden Prize, the Somerset Maugham Award and the Whitbread Prize. For the past few years his home has been in Tayport, across the Tay from Dundee, and he has taken a leading role in the academic and cultural life of that city. His book reviews appear every week in the *Herald*.

GRAEME SMITH, son of the distinguished Aberdeen journalist and author Robert Smith, has along with his colleague George MacDonald provided the *Herald* with dynamic and in-depth coverage of the North-East of Scotland. Their efforts have been rewarded with significant circulation gains in that area. A family man, he is a keen runner and a loyal supporter of Aberdeen FC. He was previously with the Edinburgh *Evening News*.

ALF YOUNG is the *Herald*'s economics editor. He was successful in two careers – in education and politics – before becoming a full-time journalist relatively late in life. He worked for Radio Clyde, the late lamented *Sunday Standard* and the *Scotsman*, before joining the *Herald* in 1986. He is a widely respected commentator on Scotland's business and industrial life and a consistent winner in the Bank of Scotland Press Awards. He lives in Strathblane.

JOHN FOWLER revived an early desultory interest to become in maturity an ardent hillwalker, since when he has scrambled over summits in Scotland and abroad. After Glasgow University and a spell as one of Her Majesty's more grudging soldiers, he became a journalist, for the last eight years as Arts Editor of the *Herald*. He has written several plays, only one of which, *Whaur's Yer Willie Wallace Noo?* caused any stir.

WILLIAM RUSSELL was born and bred in Lanark, where he attended the grammar school. After Glasgow University he served in the Intelligence Corps, learned Russian, and did his bit to try to end the Cold War. He joined the *Herald* in 1959, and moved to London as the paper's parliamentary correspondent in 1961. In 1985 he was appointed London editor. He enjoys travelling, particularly in Latin America, and he is an expert on the cinema (he is the *Herald*'s film critic) without being, as he puts it, either a movie buff or a movie bore.